MARGARETHA MONTAGU

Horse Riding Confidence Secrets.

First edition

This book was professionally typeset on Reedsy.
Find out more at reedsy.com

Contents

-

Horse Riding
Confidence Secrets

By Dr Margaretha de Klerk
(nom de plume: Margaretha Montagu)
MargarethaMontagu.com
EquineGuidedGrowth.com
Fresian Fillies Fan Club
MargarethaMontagu@gmail.com

ISBN: 9782956732426
Publisher: SemperEquuS

-

Horsemanship is the one art for which it seems one needs only practise. However, practise without true principles is nothing other than routine, the fruit of which is a strained and unsure execution, a false diamond which dazzles semi-connoisseurs often more impressed by the accomplishments of the horse than the merit of the horseman.

Francois Robichon de la Gueriniere

Invitation

Would you like to escape on a virtual visit to the sun-blessed south of France?

Join me on a virtual tour to one of the most unspoilt parts of south-west France, where you can lose yourself in the gorgeous pictures of the meadows, mountains, lakes, orchards, vineyards, lost-in-time villages, decadently delicious food and outstanding wines of this region while you listen to some of the most beautiful French chansons ever written.

Ever wondered why your self-confidence fails you when you can least afford it?

All you have to do is to subscribe to my blog, SemperEquuS' mailing list, where you will find empowering tips, motivating quotes, inspiring articles, lots of *how-to* blog posts and early-bird and last-minute special offers on my workshops. Subscribers receive a copy of my *10 Steps to Instant Self-Confidence* guide – for those stressful days - **straight from the horse's mouth!** As well as a copy of the Courageously Coping with Challenges and Change Cheatsheet and Checklist.

Reading my blog will enable you to

- Discover what is wrong with the south of France
- Read more about mindfulness meditation and find your way to a better practice
- Free yourself from your immobilising fear and deal with stress more

effectively

- Find out more about equine-assisted personal development and how to connect with horses.

Fill in your e-mail address to receive news of my workshops in the south of France with details of last-minute discounts and early bird special offers, available only to my mailing list subscribers. Your adventure starts right away, and you will shortly be off to the south of France! Your e-mail address is 100% safe, and you can unsubscribe from my mailing list at any time. You can subscribe at either of my websites: Go to MargarethaMontagu.com or EquineGuidedGrowth.com

Copyright

Dedication

I dedicate this book to my horses: my stallion Beau de la Babinière and Aurileo d'Alegria who are no longer with us, and to my soul mare Belle de la Babinière, Tess des Sources Sacrées, the Duc D'Alegria, Aurore d'Alegria and Bass des Sources Sacrées.

Foreword

Dear Reader,

I am very grateful that you have bought this book as I am sure you will benefit from it. This book was written for everyone who has ever lost their riding confidence due to an accident or a bad fall, or suffered from competition nerves. Based on sound, tried-and-tested NLP principles, it will show you step-by-step how to conquer your fear and then make your fear work for you.

Over the years, I have fallen more than once, sometimes I have broken a bone or two. Before I started using the techniques described in this book, it took a long time after each fall before I managed to get back on a horse. Months, on one occasion. Now, when I fall, assuming I am physically capable, I mostly get back on within a day or two. I say mostly because I am only human and these days it takes quite a bit longer to recover physically.

My name is Margaretha Montagu. I am an experienced medical doctor, a certified NLP practitioner, a certified counsellor, a medical hypnotherapist, an equine-assisted experiential learning coach and the author of several self-help articles, blog posts and books. I also publish a blog called SemperEquuS.

Here at our farm in the south of France, we host personal empowerment workshops with horses for riders and non-riders. Quite a large number of our workshop participants attend to increase their self-confidence with equine-assisted experiential learning and to reduce their stress levels with equine-guided meditation. Some of the techniques described in this book are used during these unmounted workshops. You are very welcome to attend one of our workshops if you need help with putting these techniques into practice. Our workshop participants work with Friesian and Irish Cob (Gypsy Vanner) horses.

Could I invite you to subscribe to my blog's mailing list? If you have already subscribed, thank you so much. If not, please do! It will enable me to continue to support you in your quest to become your best self, once you have finished reading this book. My blog aims to assist you in making the most of yourself and in providing you with the tools to do so. The blog has a distinctly French flavour, as I also share with you our life here in the south of France. You can subscribe at MargarethaMontagu.com.

I would appreciate it enormously if you would write a review for this book. A short sentence, even just one word, will be enough. It will help other people find this book so that they can benefit from reading it too.

I would also hugely appreciate it if you would let me know if you find spelling mistakes in the text. English is not my first language, so despite my best intentions, errors do slip in.

It is my dearest wish that this book will make a difference in your riding, for the better and in the long-term. This must be about the ninth edition of this book, I keep improving it according to new discoveries and the feedback that I get from comments on Facebook and my workshops. So please, let me know what you thought when you have read it or leave me a review. It is not a long book, I severely restrained myself and condensed it so that you can take it everywhere with you, especially to riding lessons, and use it as a quick reference in case of need.

Before you start reading, I want to point out that all the downloads mentioned in this book are free and that the book contains NO affiliate links. This book is my gift to you, to enable you to enjoy riding again - in all gaits.

Wishing you the greatest horse riding success!

Bien Cordialement,
Margarétha Montagu

About The Author

Dr. Margaretha Montagu
(MBChB, MRCGP, NLP cert, Med Hyp Dip and EAGALA cert level 2)

Qualifications, Interests and Experience

You only really need to read the rest of this chapter if you wonder what skills and experience I have that would make this book a worthwhile read. I may have a fair number of letters after my name, but that is not what qualifies me to write this book. It is the strategies that I had to develop to cope with what happened to me during the last ten years that makes this book worth reading.

The Past

Ten years ago, my life changed completely. I got divorced, I gave up my job as a medical doctor, I sold my house, I moved to another country, I remarried, I retrained in an entirely new discipline, and I started my own business.

In the last decade, the debilitating eye disease that threatens my sight got dramatically worse. Several unsuccessful operations have left me completely blind in one eye and with about 40% sight left in the other eye.

Somewhere along the line, during the last ten years, I started writing.

Writing was my salvation. I started small, by keeping a journal. I wrote all the pain, doubt, fear and suffering out of my system and onto the pages of my journal. Eventually, I distilled the content of my journals into books: five books so far, all equine-inspired, life-enriching and subtly French flavoured.

I wrote these books because I felt an urgent urge to share with as many people as possible how I managed to survive this insufferable decade, in case what I have learned can help others cope with equally difficult circumstances.

En plus, there is a certain satisfaction to be had from putting nearly thirty years of knowledge, training and experience down on paper.

During the last ten years, I have learned how to cope with the stress generated by insecurity. Working as a medical doctor already gave me a fair amount of insight, but it was the fear of going blind that was my most merciless instructor. Stress can do severe damage to our mental and physical health. I was no exception. Despite my eye problems, I want to live a long, happy and fulfilling life, full of purpose and meaning. To do so, I realised that I was going to have to find an effective way of coping with stress.

By trial and error, I did, and I tell you all about it in my book *Embracing Change – in 10 minutes a Day.*

The Present

Today I am the proud co-owner of a thriving business based on equine-assisted personal empowerment. My unlikely co-owners are five talented, intelligent and knowledgeable horses.

I have finally made the dream come true that inspired me to make all those changes ten years ago. I developed a whole arsenal full of tried-and-tested strategies to cope with the challenges that came my way, challenges I often have to face with a severely limited number of resources.

In my books, and during our workshops, my horses and I share these strategies with you. I always wanted to own a horse or two, so when I could no longer work as a doctor, I bought Belle de la Babinière, a stunningly handsome Friesian mare. As a companion for Belle, I bought Beau de la Babinière, a drop-dead-gorgeous Lusitano stallion. I retrained in equine-assisted personal empowerment. I now host Connect with Horses personal empowerment workshops to help my guests to be more assertive, to cope better with stress and to communicate more effectively.

Blog and Books

As I mentioned, I discovered that I liked writing, so I started a blog. I intended the blog to be a shop window showcasing our region, my horses and my workshops. It quickly became much more. Browsing my blog is indeed a bit like visiting us virtually, but it is also a library filled with articles about confidence building, problem-solving, strengthening relationships, conflict resolving and much more.

My first personal empowerment book is called *Self-Confidence made Simple: 16 Frenchwomen share their Self-esteem Secrets* (you can read a preview of this book in the last chapter.) I wrote a second book called *You ARE Good Enough!* and *Mindfulness and Meditation Options* soon followed.

I am forever writing more books. I notify subscribers to my mailing when I publish another one. Before I publish a book, I send an advanced reader's copy to each of the members of my **VIP Beta Readers Group** to find out what they think of it. I can never have too many beta readers, so if you would like to join this group, please send me an e-mail to margarethamontagu@gmail.com with "VIP Readers" as the subject.

Online Presence

Living here in deepest rural France is bliss, but one has to be careful not to become too isolated. Social media is my connection to the world beyond all these glorious sunflower fields, vineyards and woods. I have an account just about everywhere, and I would love to talk to you, in person, wherever you hang out. I adore Pinterest. I lose many hours of my life there. When I researched this book, I collected a considerable number of quotes, articles and blog posts. I share them on Pinterest (Margaretha'sMuse) and on Twitter too (@EquineGuidedMD). I am on LinkedIn (MargarethaMontagu), on Instagram (MiaMontagu) and on Patreon (Friesian Fillies Fan Club.) I have an author page on Amazon and at Goodreads, (MargarethaMontagu) and I am always in need of more followers at both these places. If you haven't come across Goodreads, have a look. I love reading even more than writing, and at Goodreads, I found my reading-tribe. I also have a Facebook page that I use as an *aide-memoire*. It is called (guess what?) Margaretha Montagu.

There is something I want you to know.

Despite all my experience, knowledge and qualifications, I am no different from you. I am far from perfect. I do not always practice what I preach. I do not have the answers to all my questions, and I do not have the solutions to all my problems. Like you, I sometimes feel that I could not possibly get back on a horse. Ever. But I hope that as you read this book and implement its suggestions, you will end up with an unshakable conviction that you can cope with whatever happens to you on or off horseback. May this conviction start knocking early, insist on being admitted, way overstay its welcome, refuse to leave and bring you the gift of God's unconditional love.

Contents

Our greatest weakness lies in giving up. The most certain way to succeed is always to try just one more time. - Thomas Edison

5. We are our own greatest enemy – we destroy our horse riding confidence by incessantly and endlessly criticising ourselves, our riding and our horses (oh yes, and our riding instructor, the weather, the sand in the arena....). Revitalise your flagging horse riding confidence by finding out **how to stop judging and criticising yourself.**

6. Use the highly-effective NLP technique of **anchoring** to boost your riding confidence, calm your nerves during a competition, enjoy a hack as you did as a child...For absolutely instant results: anchor yourself-I'll tell you exactly how

7. **Setting realistic horse riding goals** and then achieving them will do wonders for your riding confidence. Setting goals is an art and a science and unless you set your goals correctly, you will fail and destroy the little confidence you had left. This chapter explains how to set effective, S..M.A.R.T goals.

8. **A different viewpoint** can be an eye-opener. This technique is so revolutionary that I hesitate even to give a short description of it here – suffice to say, if you implement this strategy you will never look at horse riding in the same way again.

9. How will you **measure your success**? How will you know that your horse riding confidence is increasing and that you will be able to rely on it when you need it? This chapter explains how to evaluate the effect of this book on your riding confidence.

Formulate and stamp indelibly on your mind a mental picture of yourself as succeeding. Hold this picture tenaciously. Never permit it to fade. Your mind will seek to develop the picture...Do not build up obstacles in your imagination.

Norman Vincent Peale

Preparation

We have recently added a new coping strategy to our Connect with Horses personal empowerment workshops. As with equine-assisted experiential learning, equine-guided meditation and equine-led walking meditation, it is an activity that participants practice in the presence of our horses. If you are anxious about riding, this strategy is a excellent starting point. Put it in practice before you get on your horse or at any time while you are riding.

A lot has been said about how horses use breathing to connect and to communicate. Horses tend to breathe slower and deeper when they need to either calm themselves or another herd member. The question arose: "Could we possibly connect and communicate with horses by regulating our breathing?"

In my opinion, the answer is a resounding "Yes!" Not only can we calm a distressed horse by breathing slowly and deeply, but we can also be calmed ourselves by paying attention and regulating our own breathing.

First of all, we must become aware of our breathing, an automatic process most of us pay very little attention to on a day-to-day basis. Take a minute or two now and observe how quickly or slowly you are breathing. Is your breathing low (you are breathing from your belly), or high (you are breathing from your chest)? Is there a pause between your in-breath and your out-breath? Do you breathe through your mouth or your nose? It will be easier to determine your breathing speed and pattern if you put one hand on your chest and the other hand under your bellybutton. This way, you can feel which part of your body mostly moves up and down every time you inhale and exhale. Become aware of your breathing in a non-judgemental way – there is no right or wrong way to do this exercise; it is merely about observing what is happening naturally.

This is probably one of the best mindfulness exercises I know, while doing it you are 100% present in the current moment.

When we are anxious, for example, when we are scared of getting back on a horse after a fall, we change the way we breathe, without realising. Both our breathing rate and pattern change. Instead of taking deep breaths, into our lower lungs, we start to breathe superficially. We take quick, shallow breaths, into our upper lungs only. It feels as if we cannot breathe. We say that we cannot "catch our breath." This expression is not entirely accurate, because we manage perfectly well to breathe in, even if only in short, sharp breaths. The problem is that we do not breathe out properly; we breathe out in short gasps. This can lead to a condition called hyperventilation.

When we breathe, we breathe in oxygen and breathe out carbon dioxide. Fast, shallow breathing can cause the carbon dioxide levels in your bloodstream to drop too low. This, in turn, can cause quite a few uncomfortable and alarming symptoms. You may

-Have palpitations – your heart feels as if it is racing – and tightness in your chest or chest pain. This is why panic attacks are often confused with heart attacks.

-Feel lightheaded, weak, faint, dizzy and unable to think straight

-Have tingling or numbness in your fingertips or around your mouth

-Experience a sense of terror, or impending doom or death

-Have a dry mouth and feel sweaty, hot and bothered or you may have chills

-Feel nauseous and have abdominal pain or bloating
-Feel as if you are losing control

If this should happen, you can avoid a full-blown panic attack right there next to or on your horse by mindfully doing breathing exercises. Below are some breathing exercises which will help you avoid hyper-ventilation. It is important that you breathe in and out at a steady rate.

Exercise 1: Start by imagining your lungs are divided into three parts. Breathe in gently through your nose. First, imagine the lowest part of your lungs filling with air. Next, imagine the middle part of your lungs filling with air and then your lungs filling with air right to the top. Gently and slowly exhale fully and completely. Repeat the exercise three or four times.

Exercise 2: Take a deep, full breath. Exhale slowly, fully and completely. Inhale again and count from 1 to 4 (or for as long as feels comfortable). Pause for 4 seconds. Exhale slowly while counting from 1 to 4 (or for as long as feels comfortable). Pause for 4 seconds. Repeat the exercise three or four times. This is also called *square breathing.*

Exercise 3: Resting the tip of your tongue against the roof of your mouth, right behind your top front teeth. Keep your tongue in place throughout the practice. Start by exhaling completely through your mouth. Next, close your mouth, inhaling silently through your nose as you count to four in your head. Then, for seven seconds, hold your breath. Exhale from your mouth for eight seconds. This is called *4-7-8 breathing.* Repeat at least 4 times. The held breath (for seven seconds) is the most critical part of this practice.

Once you are fully conscious of your breathing rhythm and depth, pay attention to your horse's breathing speed and pattern. If your horse is anxious too, do one of the exercises and again notice your horse's breathing, to find out if there has been a change. Often your horse's breathing slows and becomes deeper too.

Whenever you feel anxious, whether you are with your horse or not, I recommend you do one of the breathing exercises above. My personal favourite is *square breathing*. It will help you to relax and can also help you fall asleep. If you find yourself in a difficult situation, do the exercise of your choice at least twice a day.

Introduction

Instant Riding Confidence? Impossible!

Instant Confidence? Isn't that a bit unrealistic? Doesn't it take years and years and years to become a confident rider?

Absolutely not! You can make your own life and that of your horse much easier by exercising your mind with as much devotion as you both exercise your bodies.

Although there are still a fair number of trainers and instructors who desperately cling to this antiquated theory, modern science has discovered that our most magnificent brains were cannily designed incorporating several useful built-in short cuts, ours to benefit from should we choose to do so.

Still don't believe me? What does the smell of freshly baked bread remind you of? Or freshly brewed coffee? Reminds me of my grand-mother's kitchen and the feeling of deep contentment I felt when I sat there at her kitchen table, sinking my teeth into a mouth-wateringly delicious, still-warm slice of bread, butter dripping down my chin.

That's a short-cut to that feeling of contentment.

The same method can be used to generate a feeling of confidence. This book will introduce you to simple but effective techniques to install short-cuts, ready to be used at any time, anywhere, instantly.

Most common reasons why riders lose their confidence

So you have mislaid your confidence?

Or had it shattered in a million pieces when you least expected it?

Or was it worn down gradually over many weeks until it has now become more or less invisible?

Or did you wake up one morning and found that, on the way to the show your confidence had completely disappeared never to reappear again?

Riders get scared for various reasons. Feel free to choose one or several reasons from the following. Or add your own private, unique misery.

You may have been hacking out perfectly confidently all your life, but you've had a recent misadventure that left you injured physically, emotionally or both.

Or you may be an accomplished rider, but you cannot handle the stress and fear of failing when competing. Nothing surprising there, we are all familiar with that sickening feeling.

Or maybe you are a beginner, and the whole size-of-the-horse, distance-to-the-ground-thing is causing you panic-attacks.

Or maybe your age or health leaves you doubting your riding abilities. You may have become afraid to handle your horse at all.

I know exactly how you feel; nervous, worried, terrified, frustrated, helpless, useless and depressed. Been there, done that.

It took me weeks to get back in the saddle after a nasty fall and months to get my confidence back. While searching desperately and impatiently for solutions, I discovered several tremendously effective mental strategies that got me confidently back into the saddle in no time at all.

This is what this book is about: saving other riders the hassle and time of doing all the trial-and-error research and present them with a list of instant, practical solutions.

The core principles of mental fitness

Whatever it is that you want to achieve with your horse and your riding, there is one fundamental concept you have to accept in all its complexity: you have to exercise your mind with as much diligence as you exercise your body.

First of all, you have to clear the deck: you have to get rid of the fear and frustration that has been accumulating over days, weeks and months. Only then can you start to rebuild your shattered confidence by exercising your mental muscles regularly and purposefully.

Your mental fitness determines how efficiently you learn; how easily you remember new information and master new skills. How effectively you can use your brain to achieve the goals you aim for is subject to your level of mental fitness.

You get mentally fit in exactly the same way as you get fit physically. By exercising your mental muscles. Daily, preferably. Otherwise, as often as you can find the time. The fitter you are mentally, the more dramatic the increase in your confidence.

There are different ways you can get fit physically. Walking, running, swimming, weight-lifting, yoga.... And of course, riding. In the same way, there are different ways you can get mentally fit. Some are easy, some are challenging. It's often the more challenging ones that have the most benefit. All serious athletes now acknowledge that physical fitness and technique is not enough.

You won't compete in an endurance race the day after the first gentle canter since you brought your horse in from the field. Similarly, you can't just read about these strategies and then expect your confidence to increase drastically. You can, however, start to see results early in your training program, spurring you on to improve your mental fitness even more.

If you don't take care of physical fitness, it's more likely you'll develop physical illness and disease. Similarly, if you don't take care of your mental fitness, you'll lose your mental capacity as you get older, or you'll experience age-related mental decline earlier in life. Both physical and mental fitness can help your body and brain work effectively together for longer. The mind-body link should never be ignored.

Any technique that promises a significant increase in your confidence without any mental effort on your part is suspicious! That's like saying you can improve your physical fitness without lifting a finger.

Even anchors, the most instantaneous of instant confidence builders, have to be installed at least once.

There is a vast variety of mental exercises at the thinking rider's disposal: mental rehearsal, anchoring, resourceful state induction, eradicating limiting beliefs with affirmations, reframing, perceptual positioning and many more...at least one to suit every rider, though most riders prefer to use their own combination of techniques.

The aim of this book

This book aims to help all riders, whether they are beginners or serious competitors, to realise their dreams.

You will learn how to optimise your unique talents and skills by harnessing the collective powers of your mind, your body, and your individual resources. The ability to build (or even re-build) your self-confidence, is essential for any rider. This information works from the inside out, resulting in a set of concrete strategies that are powerful, easy to apply, and quick to show results.

Strategies like creative visualisation and guided imagery also have a place in this book. One has to practise them a bit longer, but once they are a habit, their effect is as instant and equally spectacular. The power of suggestion to the sub-conscious mind cannot be neglected. I believe it is an essential supplement to the thinking rider's mental tool-kit.

I describe the various methods not in order of importance, but in order of personal discovery. Some of the NLP techniques, like anchoring, can be installed in a matter of minutes, and work immediately- other methods require longer mental practise, but they all benefit from repetition, as often as you can find the time.

Try out various options first. You will soon find that certain techniques work better and faster for you than others. Some may do absolutely nothing for you at all.

We are all different: there is no one-fit-all recipe. Experimenting with these methods is educational in itself, it is time well spent, for your personal benefit, but also, indirectly for the benefit of your horse.

Self-assessment

Who are you? What are you worth? As a rider? As a person?

A person's worth in this world is estimated according to the value they put on themselves.
(Jean De La Bruyere)

Let's start by getting an idea of how confident you are here and now:

Simple, Quick Self-confidence Quiz

Rate your Self-Esteem and receive feedback.

How confident are you around your horse, and around people in general? How you feel about yourself, your horse and your riding affect the way you behave in most situations. Complete the quiz below- it will only take a few minutes- to evaluate your own beliefs about yourself and to assess whether you need to work on improving your self-concept.

Instructions: Score each of the following statements using the scale below. Be objective and honest when you respond.

0 = Not at all true for me.
1 = somewhat true/true part of the time.
2 = fairly true/true half of the time.
3 = mainly true/true most of the time.
4 = True all of the time.

1. I don't feel everyone else is better than me at riding or understanding my horse.

2. I am free of shame, blame and guilt about my treatment of my horse and my riding.

3. I am a happy, carefree horse lover/rider.

4. I do not need to prove that I am as good as, or better than other riders.

5. I do not have a strong need for other people's admiration or approval.

6. Losing, or not getting the score I hoped for, does not make me feel inferior to others.

7. I am generous toward myself, my horse and other people.

8. I do not think others are better than I am because they can ride better, have more money or are more popular.

9. I make friends easily, both of the equine and the human kind.

10. I speak up about my own ideas, likes and dislikes. I don't allow my horse to walk all over me.

11. Other people's opinions or attitudes do not hurt me.

12. I do not need praise to feel good about my riding.

13. I feel happy about other people's good luck, especially if I know them well.

14. I do not find fault with my horse, my riding. the course or the judges simply because it is the fashionable thing to do.

15. I don't feel as if I should always please others, and this includes my horse.

16. I'm open and honest and not afraid of letting people see my real self. (No use trying to hide it from one's horse)

17. I am friendly, thoughtful and generous. I do not blame others - or my horse! - for my problems or mistakes.

18. I enjoy being alone with my horse.

19. I can accept compliments and gifts without feeling uncomfortable, guilty or that I do not deserve them.

20. I can admit my mistakes and defeats, to myself, my horse and

other people without feeling pain or feeling diminished in any way.

21. I feel no need to defend what I think, say or do.

22. I do not need others to agree with me or tell me that I am right.

23. I do not brag about myself, my horse or my riding.

24. I can accept constructive criticism, from both other people and from my horse!

25. I say what I mean, and I mean what I say to both my horse and the people I come in contact with.

Total Score: ________

How did it go? Some of these questions make one think.
More than 75 confirm a healthy self-concept,
50–75 implies that you would benefit from improvement
and less than 50 means there is a lot of work to be done.

We need to understand who we are so that we can understand how our horses see us.

Knowing ourselves inside out, with all our strengths and weaknesses, and accepting who we are, is truly confidence-building.

We are good at demanding the best from others, but we often go much lighter on ourselves. We allow excuses to hold us back, and then we use those same excuses to explain why we haven't become as successful as we want to be. While the expectations and demands on our time and energy usually detract from our resources, demanding more from ourselves adds to whom we are. The harder we work on ourselves, and the more excellence we demand from our actions, the more focused we will be and the better people we become because of it.

Demanding the best from ourselves is not the same as expecting perfection or never being satisfied with our own or our horse's progress. It's not about being unreasonable or trying to push ourselves beyond our true abilities. Demanding the best from ourselves is about being honest about what we can and cannot do, about learning how to break through our limits and refusing to accept excuses that limit our potential. It's about recognising our strengths, honouring our accomplishments, and always striving for excellence in all areas of our lives.

Today, take a look at your accomplishments and assess your real strengths.

Have you been pushing yourself as hard as you can? Or have you been avoiding action because it seems like too much work to step out of your comfort zones? Have you been drifting aimlessly along, resting on your laurels, rather than striving for progress? If you are honest with yourself, you may realise that you have not been pushing yourself as hard as you could, and therefore you haven't accomplished as much as you are truly capable of. Changing this is as simple as demanding the best from yourself, beginning right now.

The biggest challenge is the mastery of self. That takes place ONLY through self-discovery.

Do not be afraid to acknowledge your limitations, accept them as part of the unique being that you are. You cannot change who you are, but you can change how you perceive yourself. If you respect and care for yourself, so will other people, including your horse! But if you believe all sorts of limiting things about yourself, you will find that everyone else does too. Looking after your self-esteem is YOUR responsibility, so make sure you assess it regularly and eradicate any limiting beliefs that may have formed.

Limiting Beliefs

How to get rid of outdated, unproductive, restraining beliefs that you hold about yourself and your riding.

Why limit yourself by under-estimating your abilities?

Most of us have very rigid ideas of who we are, what we can or can't do, what we do or don't believe about horses and riding, about instructors and farriers and vets. Very few of us are willing to adjust our beliefs even in the face of overwhelming evidence to the contrary.

When our view of horses and riding is distorted by our own narrow perceptions and convictions, the choices and opportunities we have can become severely restricted. Instead of changing our beliefs, we get even more entrenched in our comfort zone and decide instead to find someone or something else to blame: our horse, for example. Or the weather, another rider, the course planner, the trainer, our instructor etc. etc.

WHY DO WE DO THIS TO OURSELVES? AND TO OUR HORSES?

Consider the immense range of convictions: likes and dislikes, wants and don't wants, can and can't dos, that you carry within you. Beliefs are views, ideas (idealistic when we are young, fatalistic as we get older) principles, judgements and decisions about ourselves, people close to us, our horses, our trainers and our community.

These ideas are often far from accurate or realistic. We had an experience. We processed it through our preferred perceptual mode, giving it a uniquely personal slant, generalising, distorting and deleting what we don't like along the way. And then we decide it is the GOSPEL TRUTH.

But our beliefs are not facts just because we decide that they are. We can change our minds. You may have been convinced, from past experience that Arab stallions are too hot to ride. Then one day, you are confronted with the sweetest, most amenable Arab stallion on the face of the earth and hey presto! You've changed your mind.

And don't confuse beliefs with values. People used to believe the earth is flat. They used to believe no one could run the mile in under 4 minutes. Your beliefs influence what you see, hear and feel in the world around you and as a result, determine the meaning you associate with an event.

We see what we want to see and hear what we want to hear. We develop selective blindness and deafness and don't even realise.

Beliefs can, therefore, act as self-fulfilling prophecies. Believe you will fail (or fall), and you will. Your beliefs, whether they are limiting or empowering, determine your actions, which in turn prove to you that your beliefs are true. Over time, as you generate more "evidence", your beliefs become increasingly ingrained and difficult to eliminate.

Our beliefs determine our expectations of ourselves and our horses. "I can't do sitting trot" is a belief, not a fact. You also used to believe in the Tooth Fairy, Father Christmas and that the moon was made of cheese. While we are aware of many of our beliefs, in general, our most influential beliefs operate below the level of our conscious awareness.

There are some beliefs that we view as absolute truths and never question – "that is just the way horses are!" A change in our beliefs can have a major impact on how we live our lives and how we react in any given situation.

Every day, a young foal tries to leap over a brook. Because he is only a young foal and the brook is bursting its banks after recent rains, he never makes it to the other side and lands in a heap in the middle of the stream. As time goes by, he gives up and stops trying. Eventually, the stream shrinks to a quarter of its original size, but the foal never tries again, not when he grows to be an agile colt nor when he becomes a powerful stallion. In his mind, the brook is still a potent river.

Our beliefs don't always match our true abilities.

This powerful stallion suffers from *learned helplessness.* Do you have the same problem with some aspects of your riding? Do you repeatedly tell yourself that you cannot jump because you had a bad fall when you were a child?

Most of us are sure that some of the things that we want to do, is impossible because of some past experience/s. But is it really that unattainable? Or do we suffer from learned helplessness like the stallion in the story?

Everyone has that earnest aspiration to succeed. One's ability to establish and accomplish goals will mould one's happiness and success over and above any skill one can master. You cannot hit the target when you cannot see it.

The foundation of your success is deciding precisely what you really and truly want, in all aspects of your life.

If every individual has that yearning to win, and if success is accessible to everybody, why then, do so few succeed? It's because only a few believe in their potential. Only a few started by defining or even acknowledging a clear, realistic goal, and honestly believe that they can achieve that goal.

Almost everyone had, at some point, gone through challenging life experiences. These experiences and encounters usually define our beliefs. The danger lies in categorising these difficult experiences as proof that one is not "good enough" in order to succeed.

You may be familiar with the concept that your beliefs create your reality, but have you explored this idea further? What does it really mean that your beliefs create your reality? A belief is a thought that has been repeated in your mind so many times that you know it to be "true." Sometimes the things we believe really are true, but other times we have tricked ourselves into believing something is true, even if it isn't. These illusory "truths" are reinforced because our actions day to day create "proof" that reinforces the belief.

Take, for example, the belief that you are not strong enough or talented enough to achieve the riding success you crave. If you believe this about yourself, you will feel no incentive to try to succeed so you will avoid taking action that could make you successful. If you do somehow manage to overcome your self-doubt and start working toward a specific goal, the slightest obstacle you encounter will convince you that your original belief was correct: you don't have what it takes! Your every thought and action will be transmitting energy into the universe that says, "I want to be successful and happy....but I can't be successful and happy!" The opportunities and abundance you asked for, become invisible. You have now cemented the belief in your mind because you feel incapable of making progress, so surely you must NOT be worthy of the goals you aim to achieve.

To destroy your limiting beliefs (whether about horses, horse riding or anything else) you need to be willing to question their validity. You need to be ready to face the fears you have, the self-doubts, the beliefs that you are not worthy of success and find out WHY you believe those things. Once you have identified your limiting beliefs, it's a simple matter to change them and replace them with more realistic affirmative beliefs. Once you start to question your beliefs and gradually change them, you create "proof" that the new beliefs are true – which eradicates your previous limiting beliefs!

Beliefs are powerful and affect our decisions, feelings, and actions. Although you depended on a specific set of suppositions regarding your riding and understanding of your horse for so many years, those particular beliefs can be adjusted or changed. Start changing them now!

Do you think of yourself as a classical rider, a show-jumper, a hunter, a natural horsemanship disciple - or do you believe you will never be able to do more than hacking out? Are you a failure or a winner? Are you a "natural" or an "imposter"? Become aware of all the labels you attach to yourself.

Where did these labels originate? Did they come from you? Your parents? An instructor? An experience? Look at each label you can identify with regards to horses and riding and determine where each one originated.

And are there any labels that you are holding on to rather desperately? Do your labels serve a purpose?

Does believing that your horse cannot jump protect you from facing your fear of falling off?

Which, if any, of these beliefs, would you be willing to question and possibly give up? Ask yourself the following 10 questions:

1. What kind of rider do you believe yourself to be: excellent, useless or average?
2. Do you have a great seat, a hopeless seat, or somewhere in the middle?
3. Are you too thin, too fat, too muscular or just right?
4. Are you smart, dumb, slow or average?
5. Are you a concentrated rider, or do you think of yourself as generally unfocused?
6. Are you capable of great things, pretty average in your riding potential or meant to stick to hacking?
7. Is life unfair, or were you born lucky?
8. Are you receiving all that you deserve from life?
9. Are people (and horses!) in generally trustworthy?
10. Do you chat easily to people or are you always an outsider?

Take a moment and consider this: Each answer you gave was a belief, no more, no less. It was based solely on your perception of yourself and on your interpretation of past experiences.

If we assume that all riders have some way of sabotaging their achievements, which is your favourite method (choose one or more)?

Procrastination, impatience, inability to say no, delegation allergy, motivation failure, self-doubts.....add your own.

Once we firmly believe in something, we tend to ignore evidence to the contrary and focus only on those events that reinforce that belief. Because beliefs are so much part of who we are, and how we act, they can be buried very deep within us.

You may like to consider getting support from others to help you become more self-aware. The rewards will be worth the effort, once you're free of any self-imposed limitations. Ask a friend/ fellow rider or trusted instructor if they have noticed any limiting beliefs that you impose on yourself.

Most of our beliefs originate from the time we were children. They are not based on fact, but on our perception of events at the time they were formed. We modelled people who played a significant role in our lives – parents, instructors, older siblings, pony club friends, famous riders and yes, even horses.

We made generalisations based on single traumatic experiences, assuming things ALWAYS happens this way. Or through trial-and-error, we subscribe to those beliefs that please us, avoided pain or provided safety. We accept what we were told about ourselves – "you are incapable of ever becoming a competent rider" OR "you can achieve whatever you choose to." Some of our limiting beliefs are based on complete misinterpretations of past events.

How can I use this?

Can we change our beliefs? Of course. Changing them is easy. Unearthing them is the difficult part.

The first step to changing a belief is to become consciously aware of the belief and its impact on your life. Beliefs can be changed when we are confronted with irrefutable information that proves our current beliefs are inaccurate. Or when we purposefully decide to change a belief and consciously notice its positive effects until it becomes a way of life. Initially, you may find it a bit difficult to stick to a new belief. However, if you keep at it, you will find that it becomes easier as your performance improves dramatically.

Once you've exposed your limiting belief, you can then choose another one to replace it with that will be more useful to you. We take our beliefs for granted and look for evidence that ties in with them, proving us right all along. So, once you've chosen your new belief, or affirmation, you can deliberately look for evidence that backs it up, and you'll find that the new belief will soon become second nature to you.

Use affirmations to clear away any limiting beliefs you might have been holding, and your confidence and self-esteem will grow exponentially.

Re-condition your mind

An affirmation is an emphatic statement that you make to yourself. Everyone uses affirmations, intentionally or unintentionally. You wake up in the morning, jump out of bed and exclaim "I feel great". That is a positive affirmation. You drag yourself out of bed in the morning and whimper "I feel rotten". That is a negative affirmation. Both statements determine the emotional state you are in and affects your confidence levels. Our self-talk, our inner critic, is important because it directly affects our conscious and subconscious mind.

We can use affirmations to build our self-esteem. We can use them to control our fear and anxiety, for stress management; and to increase our horse riding confidence. We can use them to improve our riding, our relationship with our horse, our ability to perform under stress. Affirmations are used successfully in all areas of personal growth and self-improvement.

Good affirmations should:

-Imply that you have already accomplished your goal, even though you have not. "I am confident that I can jump a clear round NOW" is superior to and will work better than "I am becoming confident" or "I will be confident."

-Be in your own, personal language, using the vocabulary and grammar you usually use to express yourself.

-Incorporate as many of your senses as you can. Add imagery to it. This will make your affirmation significantly more effective. Do this by taking one of your affirmation and instead of saying the affirmations, close your eyes and imagine yourself doing or being what the affirmation asserts. Use all five of your senses. Imagery amplifies the power of the affirmation.

-Be combined with a "trigger" a specific song/ sound ex "I will survive!" a colour, an object like a rose quartz crystal, an NLP anchor or a perfume like lavender essential oil.

-Be combined with other tools ex guided imagery or hypnosis.

Affirmations are useful to counter your inner critic. When you catch yourself saying something negative to yourself, develop an affirmation that counteracts the negative thought and start using it until you feel differently about yourself. Let's say you are working on a specific riding skill but cannot master it.

Your confidence plummets, and you catch yourself thinking "I can't do this. I bit off more than I can chew. I'm just not smart enough." If this negative thinking is allowed to persist, it will guarantee failure. Instead, make up some affirmations to counter this destructive way of thinking. For example, you might use "I feel confident, I am a success, I a good rider and getting better every day". Write your affirmations on memory cards and repeat each affirmation five times three times per day until you feel better about yourself and have mastered the skill.

Choose new positive statements to replace the old negative ones. Your new affirmation should contain all the essential components mentioned above - make it personal by using the word 'I', make it in the present tense by using the word 'am' and include a positive statement like, ' I am a great rider'. The new belief doesn't have to be true yet. Here are a few examples:

I have completely discarded any thoughts of failure that I used to have with regards to my riding.

I do everything necessary to achieve my riding goals

I have no unnecessary anxiety about riding or competing.

I find it easy to discard negative thoughts and attitudes about myself, my horse and my riding.

I always think of myself in a totally positive way.

I expect to succeed at any new riding skill I plan to acquire because I am a naturally successful person.

I am tenacious and persevere with all my efforts towards riding success.

I become steadily more confident about my riding with each day that passes.

I like myself, and I'm pleased with everything I have achieved so far with my horse and my riding.

When repeating the affirmations, put some feeling into it and think about what you are trying to accomplish. Adding emotion strengthens affirmations.

Do your affirmations soon after you wake up as it will help focus your day. Do your affirmations just before going to sleep as it will be working in your subconscious mind all night.

Do not become impatient. Commit to using your affirmations for at least 30 days. If what you are trying to change is more complicated and long-standing, you will need more than 30 days.

As you use more and more intentional affirmations – written, spoken, read and recorded – they will become part of your lifestyle. Affirmations are already working for (or against!) you. Select only the ones you want to live by. If your current convictions are dis-empowering, you can intentionally change them to ones that will make your soul soar.

Whenever the old belief surfaces, say to yourself 'Stop, delete that thought'! You can even visualise a computer screen with these words appearing on it to assist the deletion process. Now repeat your new positive version to yourself. At this point, create a mental image of yourself successfully carrying out the new positive behaviour to reinforce the whole process.

Repeat this exercise continuously so that your new positive belief becomes firmly installed in your thought processes. In this way, you will improve your confidence and success in future outcomes.

How do I create a mental image?

When you do something you have done a hundred times before, something you and your horse are very good at, you feel calm and confident and completely relaxed. You have a clear idea of what you and your horse are capable of, you know you can do it, it's effortless.

Remember the last time you and your horse outdid yourselves. See everything that you saw, hear everything that you heard and feel everything that you felt - touch and emotions, and if there were any strong smells, like freshly cut grass, or tastes, like the blueberry gum you were chewing just beforehand, remind yourself of this too. Take several minutes to remember the whole event in as much detail as you can.

Next, do the same thing again but this time daydream into the future. If it is a competition, imagine the weather on the day, the sound of the crowd cheering, the sound of your horse's hooves, the smell of leather - include as much sensory detail as you can. Notice how confident you look and feel; notice how well-behaved and obliging your horse is. Take as long as you need to fully imagine the experience.

Does this work? Most definitely!! After all, there's not much point in preparing for success unless you're also prepared to be successful!

Strengths and Weaknesses

How to take full advantage of your strengths and exploit your limitations for a lasting confidence boost

Our greatest weakness lies in giving up. The most certain way to succeed is always to try just one more time. - Thomas Edison

One of the best practises you can adopt if you want to ride better is the process of inner reflection. Learn how to see through your perceptions and discern which ones are serving you and which ones are holding you back. Learn how to get in touch with your intuition and use the signals it sends (like gut feelings).

Stop fooling yourself into believing things that keep you from expressing your uniqueness and start pushing yourself to believe things that increase your self-esteem. Take off the rose-coloured glasses and begin assessing yourself with brutal honesty. Only then will you understand the quickest way to release your potential and determine the actions needed to be a successful rider.

Are you telling yourself that you're working hard on your goals when in fact you are just spinning your wheels and trying to stay busy? Are you convinced that you don't have as much chance or opportunity as others do? Are you telling yourself that the obstacle you face is too big or too imposing to overcome? Do you promise yourself that someday soon, just not today, you'll begin taking action to get what you want? Are you waiting for your fear to diminish or for your confidence to grow? No matter what you are telling yourself, be willing to question whether it's the "truth" or not. Just because it seems to be so, doesn't mean it is.

Use the Swot Analysis to identify your unique strengths and weaknesses. Decide how to take full advantage of your talents and how you can best limit the influence of your shortcomings.

Armed with this knowledge, you can work out how to make the most of the opportunities that come your way and how to minimise the impact of any threats.

The SWOT analysis - for Horse Riders

Originally, this technique was developed as a tool to determine a business's viability and improve its productivity. It soon became apparent that it can be used as efficiently by athletes and coaches, in fact, by anyone who wants to get a balanced overview of their assets, skills and opportunities.

Riders can use this method for their own benefit, but we can just as easily apply it to the strengths, weaknesses and opportunities of their horses. The bottom line here is to keep the four components in balance and not emphasise one component like your weaknesses or the threats you face, more than the others.

Aiming for balance in riding should not just be relevant to your riding technique, but also to your attitude to horse riding, to your horse, and to life in general.

Never forget that the rest of your life influence your riding: the time you can spend with your horse, the energy and money you have available....balance this with all the other demands for your attention, otherwise, you will soon BURN OUT! We are only human; we have our limitations.

Strengths, weaknesses, opportunities and challenges

• List your Strengths, and don't be economical- most riders are hard-working, determined, motivated (got to be to get up and clean stables before work in mid-winter) persistent, courageous- go on, list them all. Rate each on a scale of one to 10, 10 being the highest score. Take motivation, for example. If your motivation is a bit on the low side, think of ways you can increase it: reading inspiring books/ watching similar video's, saying affirmations, using self-hypnosis etc.

• Do the same with your weaknesses – and since most riders are perfectionists and intensely self-critical, the list should soon be long enough! Once again rate each, and decide how you can minimise or limit the effect of each.

• List all the Opportunities you can think of: a good instructor in the immediate vicinity, your husband who helps you muck out, a friend that looks after your horse when you are away, a sweet, brilliant horse....all the things we usually forget to be thankful for. Again, rate each and consider how you can amplify the benefit you can get from each.

•Threats, whether perceived or real, internal or external, are next –list, rate and dis-empower.

Incorporate your findings into your goal-setting method- the SMART method is the best- to get the most from this exercise. More about goal-setting later.

Once you have assessed your abilities and skills, and the relative strength of each, raise your estimation of them all by at least 15%. We underestimate ourselves. When faced with a problem, start by focusing on your strengths and opportunities. This will take your attention off the negative aspects and onto your riding skills and achievements.

"What's the worst thing that could possibly happen? What is the worst case scenario?" Instead of placing too much emphasis on potential disaster, we should protect our self-esteem by concentrating on finding functional and constructive solutions instead of wasting our energy by worrying unnecessarily.

Ask yourself if, by this time next year, you will even remember this incident. Keep things in proper perspective: your fear will evaporate.

If at any time you discover an undercover negative thought wheedling its way into your mind, deliberately and consciously let go of it – NOW!

Immediately replace it with a positive thought/ affirmation/ quotation. Put a small photo/ object in your wallet that generates a positive emotion in your mind: a photo of your horse, an amulet, ribbon or a medal. Each time you see or touch it, it will be like flicking the switch from negative to positive: an instant feeling of well-being or even...instant confidence!

Your inner voices will always be with you: friend or foe, optimist of pessimist, devil or saint. It's up to you to decide which one you are going to listen to.

Self-critisism

Resurrect your flagging confidence: How to stop judging and criticising yourself

How many times have your own thoughts worked against you? Maybe you turned a niggling worry into a major anxiety attack, or maybe you let fear hold you back from doing something you really wanted to do. The way you see the world around you determines the way you feel about yourself, your potential and your progress. A perception of a life full of limitations will convince you that you can't move forward. A perception of lack or need can convince you that your life is empty and devoid of opportunities. A perception of injustice will convince you that you cannot win, that you'll always lose.

What would happen if you changed these perceptions from negative to positive?

We often suffer from covert perfectionism and an insidious need to control. This limits our ability to enjoy and achieve our goals. Judging and criticising yourself destroys your self-confidence. Use this method to stop putting yourself down.

1. Meet Dr Jekyll and Mr Hyde: your Internal Coach vs your Internal Critic

We all have voices in our heads, that predicting doom and gloom from morning to night.

You are probably now thinking of your aunt Agnes who got herself admitted to a mental institution when she mentioned these voices to her neighbour. We are not talking about hearing other people's voices in your head, but about hearing your own. Everyone talks to themselves, silently either in an encouraging or discouraging way. Luckily, most of us manage to exist without our voices causing us to land up in a mental hospital.

Our internal voice exists for a simple but important reason; its job is to protect us from danger. Regretfully, our internal critic can also be an incorrigible cynic to a fault, always expecting the worst to happen.

You are thinking negatively and listening to your inner critic when you put yourself down, criticise yourself for errors, doubt your abilities, or expect inevitable failure.

Believing your inner critic can damage your self-confidence, harm your horse riding performance and paralyse your mental AND physical skills.

The problem with this is that negative self-talk tends to pop into our consciousness, do a good bit of damage and pop right out again. We hardly notice the significance of what just happened. Our internal critic is a cunning and devious creature, influencing us without us noticing it.

Some of my clients have named their negative inner voice Cruella de Ville, the Wicked Witch of the west, or Mr Hyde. Some say it sounds like the voice of their mother or father, or a strict teacher or riding instructor...what does yours sound like?

Since we are barely aware of this intruder, we do not challenge its assumptions or predictions. We believe everything we hear and then amplify its harmful effect.

2. Become aware...of Mr Hyde

To counteract our internal critic with our internal coach, we have to notice and observe our inner voices and thoughts and become aware of the running commentary going on inside our heads.

The easiest way to learn how to manage your inner coach/critic is by noticing and analysing any stressful riding related situations (and your thoughts at the time) you encounter and writing it all down in your horse riding Training Log.

The real benefit of using a Log/Diary/Journal becomes apparent if you do this for one or two weeks. When you become aware that you are criticising yourself about your riding, note all these negative thoughts, worries and fears in your training log. Logging your negative thoughts for a reasonable period will allow you to see patterns emerge in your way of thinking and talking to yourself.

When you analyse your log at the end of this period, you will be able to identify the most common and the most damaging patterns. Tackle these as a priority, using affirmations as described in the affirmations chapter. These patterns may also reveal any limiting beliefs that you are harbouring.

3. Resuscitate Dr Jekyll

The next step in dealing with negative self-talk is to confront the damaging words/thoughts that you have identified while keeping a log. Look at every thought and idea you wrote down and rationally challenge it. Ask yourself whether the thought is reasonable and realistic: Does it stand up to scrutiny?

When reviewing your log, you may have discovered that you often think about one of the following:

1. Fear of Falling/ Injury

2. Doubts that your riding performance will not be good enough

3. Concern that things outside your control will undermine your efforts

4. Worries about other people's reactions to your efforts- what will other people say?

Now decide if any of these hold any truth:

· **Fear of Falling/ Injury**: Have you trained and educated yourself and your horse as thoroughly as you reasonably could to enable you and your horse to do your best on the day of the competition? Have you planned, prepared and mentally rehearsed? If you have done all of these, and you are still seriously worried, are you setting yourself unattainably high standards?

· **Anxiety about performance**: Do you have the training that a reasonable person would think is needed to perform/ compete successfully? Have you planned appropriately? Do you have all the information you may need? Have you cued your support team appropriately? If you have not, then get to it. If you have, then you are well prepared to give the best performance that you ever have.

· **Concern about issues outside your control** (like the weather!): Do you have a contingency plan or a suitable alternative coping strategy? Have you thought through and limited all likely complications? If so, you will be well prepared to handle potential problems.

· **Worry about other people's reaction**: If you are prepared, and you do the best you can, then what other people have to say is irrelevant. Often, the best thing to do is to rise above undeserved criticism.

When you challenge negative thoughts rationally, you should be able to see quickly whether the thoughts are unrealistic or whether they have some substance to them.

Where there is some substance, take appropriate action. In these cases, your inner critic has been an early warning system showing where you need to direct your attention.

So what next? Wake up your internal coach so that he/she can contribute by repeating positive affirmations to you:

· **Fear of Falling/ Injury/ Inadequate Performance**: "We are well trained and prepared for this performance/ competition. I have thought through and am equipped for all possible eventualities. We will do a splendid job."

· **Problems issues outside your control**: "We have thought through everything that might reasonably go wrong and have planned how we can handle all likely contingencies. Everyone is ready to help where necessary. We are prepared to react with flexibility to unusual events."

· **Worry about other people's reaction**: "We are well-prepared and are doing the best we can. I will rise above any unfair criticism in a professional way."

4. Aim for Excellence, not perfection

Don't be afraid of failures: take them in your stride and move on. Say to yourself that you will succeed the next time. Never make the mistake of allowing your failures to overwhelm you. They will force you into hiding and destroy your self-confidence.

Shrug off your failures as something inconsequential, and take on a new challenge.

Of course, you must learn from your mistakes, and be realistic about your abilities. People who try to over-reach often fail.

When it comes right down to it, you have a choice in how you view any situation, challenge, goal or opportunity. There are two sides to every coin - heads or tails, positive or negative. You can choose to see the potential or the difficulties. You can choose to focus squarely on the blessings or the hardships. You can absorb life-changing lessons, or add one more negative experience to your list of woes. Every moment holds a simple choice: let your perceptions empower you or hinder you. Which will you choose today?

Mastering challenging situations will increase your self-confidence. You will acquire new skills, and you will know that you can handle challenging circumstances.

Becoming aware of your inner critic helps you understand that disruptive thinking, unpleasant memories and misinterpretation of situations can interfere with your performance and damage your self-confidence.

Aim for Excellence, NOT Perfection.

And give yourself a break. And your horse too.

Anchors

For absolutely instant confidence: anchor yourself. At the end of this section, you will understand what an anchor is and how to use it to remain calm and perform at your best

What's an anchor? Apart from the obvious?

An anchor is a trigger that generates a specific state of mind. Something sets you off- a smell, an old, forgotten song, a faded photograph... and suddenly you are back there, experiencing it all as if it was yesterday: the cheering crowd, the pouring rain, your horse's hooves splashing in the mud...that feeling of triumph, victory, intense satisfaction...it could have been yesterday.

You can use an object, like a smooth stone or a photograph, to awaken a certain feeling, or you can use something closer to home... For example, touching a thumb to an index finger while holding the reins could be an anchor that will make you feel more confident in the saddle.

Some anchors are old friends. The smell of freshly baked bread may instantly take you back to your childhood. A certain song may remind you of a particular relationship. These anchors work automatically, and you may not even be aware of them. Anchoring means to associate an internal, emotional response with some external trigger.

We are affected by anchors every day. A particular anchor triggers a good mood, another a bad one. One anchor can make us feel confident and resourceful, another just hopeless and inadequate.

Anchors have become embedded gradually and insidiously. We often think that our moods occur by chance. Not true. Moods are often triggered by external stimuli.

In the very same way, you can install an anchor to trigger a supremely confident mental state and then fire the anchor whenever you need an instant boost of confidence, like the moment you ride into the arena to ride your dressage test.

It is the process by which a memory, a feeling or some other response is associated with (anchored to) something else.

Anchoring is a natural process that usually occurs without our awareness. For example, when you were young, you undoubtedly participated in family activities that gave you great pleasure. The pleasure was associated with the activity itself, so when you think of the activity or are reminded of it, you tend to re-experience some pleasurable feeling. In this way, anchors are reactivated or, triggered.

The smell of hay, leather and saddle soap immediately transports me back to the stables where I learned to ride as a child, bring with them a warm glow of happiness and excitement.

Different types of anchor

- Anchors can be visual-you can see them,
- Auditory-you can hear them,
- Gustatory-you can taste them,
- Olfactory-you can smell them,
- or kinaesthetic-you feel them.

Visual Anchors

You can use visual anchors to anchor a resourceful, relaxed state that you can trigger whenever you feel anxious in the saddle. For example, you could use a ring to anchor being calm and confident. But then you must always wear it! The anchor always has to be there for you to access. You can also use a tattoo, a mole, a scar or a good luck charm.

Auditory Anchors

You can use a sound as an anchor, a certain song or piece of music, someone's voice, your own voice, the rhythm of your horse's hooves. Many people have used whistling as an anchor - they whistle when they feel afraid! Repeating a mantra or an affirmation out loud can also be an anchor.

Kinaesthetic Anchors.

Touching or pinching yourself in an unobtrusive place, like an earlobe, or making a circle with your thumb and index finger are effective kinaesthetic anchors. You can choose a site and treat it like an acupressure point - pressing on it to fire the required state.

Olfactory Anchors.

Aromatic oils, soap, dried lavender...whatever takes your fancy.

Taste-related Anchors.

Specifically flavoured chewing gum or strongly flavoured mints...chocolate, chocolate, and chocolate.

You can also use a combination of anchors such as seeing a particular symbol in your mind's eye, hearing the words "I am Calm and Relaxed" and touching your right knee.

Install your own - it's easy!

DIY Anchoring

Installing an anchor means producing the stimuli (visual, auditory, tactile, etc.) when the resourceful state is experienced intensely, so that the resourceful state is connected to the anchor.

Activating or firing the anchor means to set off the anchor so that the resourceful state re-occurs automatically. For example, touching the knuckle of the left hand after the anchor has been established so that this action produces the resourceful state.

Anchors are used to produce the state of mind or mood you need for a given situation. You enter the arena calm and relaxed. You control your nerves. You turn on the enthusiasm you need to master a new skill.

1. Start by deciding on the state you want to anchor. You have all the resources you require to experience whatever state you want. You can recall memories when you have experienced the required state. Recall them vividly using all five of your senses. You can recall any memories of being extremely calm and confident to get the resource state for your anchor. You might recall being calm and relaxed on holiday, for example, or from a time when you were at home enjoying your leisure time.

2. Choose an anchor (visual, auditory or kinaesthetic) that you wish to trigger the resourceful, confident state. It is useful to choose an anchor that does not involve moving your hands, as they may be holding the reins when you need to fire your anchor.

3. Recall a memory or imagine a situation when you were supremely confident, as vividly a possibly, using all five your senses.

4. Activate/fire (ex. pinch your left earlobe) the anchor when the memory/experience is at its most vivid and intense.

5. Release the anchor (let go of your earlobe) when the experience begins to fade. If you keep applying the anchor when the experience is fading, then you will anchor a drop in confidence!

6. Do something completely different- open your eyes ... count down from 10, ask the time or do sit-ups to break state and distract yourself.

7. Repeat the steps 3-6 several times, each time making the memory more vivid, more detailed and more precise. You strengthen the anchor by installing it at the emotional peak of several such experiences.

8. Apply the anchor and check that the required state occurs.

9. Check the anchor the next day to ensure it is permanent.

There you have it: Instant confidence!

NLP anchoring, like any new skill, requires a certain amount of practice. When you've learned to time your anchoring correctly, you should be able to anchor a response with only one attempt.

In the meantime, enjoy the pleasure of practising a new skill that will provide you and your horse with many happy hours. With experience, you will be able to effectively and appropriately anchor responses without even thinking about it, which is the ultimate goal.

An effectively established anchor will last until some stronger emotional event intervenes to weaken the response. If this happens, simply re-establish the anchor in the same manner.

Goal Setting

One of the BEST confidence-building tools ever developed

If you don't know what port you are sailing to, no wind is favourable. Seneca 'The Younger'

Would it surprise you to know that your self-confidence (the value you place on yourself) will determine whether you reach your goals or not?

It will also determine how your horse perceives and responds to you. The opposite is equally true: Setting and achieving realistic riding goals will boost your self-esteem substantially. Don't believe me? Just think about the last time you struggled to master a new riding skill- like the sitting trot, or shoulder-in, or getting your horse to stand still so you can get on. At the very point of exasperation, when you are at your wit's end, if you persevere despite being sorely tempted to give up...Suddenly, miraculously, it all falls into place –what a feeling!

Did you feel smart, surprised, rewarded, fulfilled, elated, and as if you were going to explode with pride? Did you feel like you could easily build on this achievement? That's how you'll feel every time you set and achieve a personal goal. It would be even more satisfying if you focused your energies purposefully onto achieving something specific and concrete.

At the end of this section, you will know how to set realistic goals, and you will understand how setting and achieving objectives maximises your self- confidence

Your self-esteem, awareness, ability to communicate with horses and people, energy and responsibility can all be amplified by your use of goal setting. Developing and maintaining our self-esteem is one of the challenges we all face in life. Confidence comes from knowing that we can do what we want to do. It results from experience, the experience of meeting goals successfully. We must have some way to evaluate an experience, some way to know whether it was good or bad. This is where goal-setting comes in. Setting realistic goals, working toward them and finally achieving them are superb learning experiences. We feel good about ourselves and our horses when we meet our goals. Our horses pick up on our sense of well-being and respond by offering cooperation and trust. Which in turn, makes it easier for us to reach our next goals, and so the effect soon snowballs, to the delight of both ourselves and our horses.

Goals give purpose and direction to your journey through life with your horses. Setting goals is not a complicated process; it merely requires a little work and planning. Practise setting goals for your riding, and the habit will carry over into the rest of your life. Goals can be big or small, old or new, on-going or once-off: learning new dressage skills, trail-riding in national parks, making new friends for horse-related activities, showing at local shows, breeding, buying a first horse, competing in endurance riding, pleasure riding on the beach, re-training Thoroughbreds off the track, buying a saddle that fits correctly, driving miniature horses, teaching a horse to stand still at the mounting block, eventing on ponies, healing a lame horse, horse camping, volunteering at a therapeutic riding program, or adults taking up riding for the first time or after a long time away.

We all have goals, whether we know it or not. We have goals to keep our current horse, or to get a different/another one. We have goals to master a specific riding skill or purchase that new saddle we need. An important distinction, however, is that supremely confident riders are very intentional and focused on their goals, while many of the rest of us are not.

Riders who realise their dreams know that the wording, structure, timing and format of a goal can make its attainment much easier – or far more difficult. They understand the essential skills for setting their goals and how to design goals that create success.

Goal setting techniques are used by top-level athletes of all disciplines, including riders. Goals give you long-term vision and short-term motivation. They focus your attention and help you to organise your time and your resources so that you can make the most of your opportunities.

Although I knew about, and even occasionally used the goal setting procedure, I severely underestimated the potential of this powerful method to improve my riding technique AND increase my riding enjoyment. Too much hassle, I thought. I have since been converted, not only by my own experience but also by the overwhelmingly positive reaction from my clients.

When I bestride him, I soar, I am a hawk. He trots the air, the earth sings when he touches it, the basest horn of his hoofs is more musical than the pipe of Hermes...When bestride him I soar, I am a hawk... ~ William Shakespeare

Goal setting is a useful tool for getting back in the saddle. All riders should set SMART goals. Otherwise, the goals will intensify the frustration of not riding as well or as often as desired. For the recreational rider, the goals may be the amount of time you will spend riding. Setting a goal gives you something tangible to work towards. You are more likely to succeed by saying, “I will ride twice a week,” rather than saying, “I will try to ride more often.” Having a tangible goal gives you a sense of accomplishment. Even if you only take a lesson a month, it will give you specific goals to work on each time you ride. Be sure to pick an instructor that is supportive and understanding of your time limitations and commitment level. The most beneficial aspect of setting a goal is that as you try to reach it, you will develop the habit of riding.

By setting sharp, clearly defined goals, you can measure and take pride in the achievement of those objectives and so increase your self-confidence. Supremely Confident Riders know that setting and achieving goals, however small and insignificant, boost their confidence on a day to day basis. Each time you realise a purposefully set objective, your confidence in your own ability grows.

SMART GOALS are:

SPECIFIC: State each goal as a positive, unambiguous statement. To reach your goals, your brain must know what you are trying to accomplish. Never word a goal with vague terms like “some” or “a little bit”, or “more”. Be specific! Your brain will help you accomplish almost anything if it knows precisely what you are aiming for.

Realistic goals are SIMPLE. Many people describe their goals in complex terms and by making endless lists. Any ONE of the points on the list is a great goal, but the combination becomes overwhelming and the brain gets confused.

Worthwhile goals are SIGNIFICANT. No one can muster the enthusiasm, hard work and courage necessary to learn dressage if they don’t care for that sort of riding. A worthwhile goal is one you really, really, REALLY want! It's something that will change your approach to riding, enhance your riding pleasure, and make you confident and proud.

Reachable goals are STRATEGIC. High achievers know that the best goals bring many benefits, all at one time. Riding four times a week will:

1) feel great!
2) help you lose weight.
3) improve your relationship with your horse
4) get you both fit
5) speed up your progress
6) increase your energy and stamina, and
7) increase your confidence.

Design your goals to strategically impact as many areas of your life as possible. You'll have more reasons to reach your goal and more excitement when you do!

SHARED. We are far more likely to stick to our plan and reach our goals if we know our friends and family support us. Being part of a team increases our determination, our stamina, and our courage. Find a support team and a coach who will encourage you every step of the way.

MEASURABLE: A goal without a measurable outcome is just a pipe-dream. You can't achieve a pound of "happiness" or 6 inches of "self-esteem", but you CAN have a riding lesson once a week. "What gets measured, gets done." Define your goals in terms of height, weight, pounds, inches, or hours. Then measure your progress until you achieve your desired outcome.

ATTAINABLE: Make sure it fits in with your current work, family and financial commitments and are CONSISTENT WITH YOUR VALUES. One of the biggest reasons people fail to achieve their goals is that they have conflict between their desires and their values. Make sure your goals are consistent with your religious and moral beliefs, and with other goals that you have. Internal conflict will undermine your performance, every time!

RELEVANT and RATIONAL. To reach your goal, you will need a plan, a path, and a vehicle for getting there. Your goals must make sense! When you explain them to friends and family, your goals should create excitement, draw support and encouragement. Your goals should be just out of reach, but not out of sight! You want to stretch to be your best, not strain after impossible dreams. Set goals you CAN and WILL achieve!

TIME-DEFINED: Aim to achieve the various stages of your goal according to a preconceived time-scale. TANGIBLE. Choose goals that you can see, hear, smell or touch. Go for things you will enjoy and that you can clearly visualise. The brain has a hard time going for "financial security", but it can visualise a bank statement with lots of large numbers on it! Define your goals and WRITE them down. Write a short description of your goals every single morning, as a personal reminder of your priorities and your objectives.

The act of writing your goals down vastly increases your chance of success. Write it down! Then, keep your notes where you can see and read them every day. Plotting out your goals in this manner will make you aware of the skills, financial aid and time you will need along the way. Develop short and mid-term goals to help you build those skills. You will begin to make decisions based on whether or not those choices will be beneficial to your long-term goals.

Commit to your goals

Are you one in that high percentage of people who every New Year's Eve thinks 'a new year, a new start - I'm going to do things differently'.

So, you tell yourself you mean it this time. You promise yourself that you'll lose weight, or make more time for your horse, start your own home-based business or even only to obtain information on goal setting. While these are all very noble personal goals, surveys have shown that within two days of setting New Year's resolutions, most people will have broken them or they will have fallen by the wayside.

Along with motivation and a deep commitment to change, you also need awareness and discipline to make long-lasting, meaningful change. There's a story from ancient Greece about a general who landed his troops on the beach, then burned his ships. He wanted each soldier to know there was no turning back, no retreat, no alternative to victory.

Once your goal is clear, emotionally commit to achieving it. There are no alternatives. Never be afraid to review your goals, evaluate whether you are still 100% committed to them, and re-commit to achieving them. If your values or your choices have changed, change your goals accordingly, and be honest about it! And if your goal still fits, strive to reach it with all your heart!

Last year I made a list of things that I resolved to do...I'll use that list again this year...It's still as good as new! Anonymous

Celebrate every intermediate victory, however small! And celebrate each milestone! Reward yourself for each goal you reach. Celebrate every step toward your goal! When you get discouraged or have doubts, your record of past successes will quickly get you back on track.

Remember, 'if you can imagine it, you can achieve it.' Any goal that truly fires your imagination and fills your heart with joy is reachable!

You now have an efficient tool to help you increase your self-confidence exponentially: SETTING SMART GOALS. It is easy, it

is rewarding, it is motivating and inspiring, so...

START TODAY!

Staying motivated to reach your gaols is not always easy. Here are five practical ways to maximise and maintain your horse riding motivation:

What is the secret of staying motivated, even when it feels as if you are getting nowhere with your riding or training of your horse?

Have you ever wondered how some horse riders seem to stay motivated so effortlessly?

How do they manage to get up in the pitch-dark on a freezing winter morning to muck out...and whistle happily while they do it?

If you've ever had a hard time getting or staying disciplined to muck out, or get back on or try an exercise one more time, you may have been struggling with a lack of motivation. Motivation and discipline usually go hand-in-hand for riders and horses, because without motivation, it is nearly impossible to become disciplined. Ironically, once you become disciplined, you rarely need to be motivated to keep your life running smoothly.

Discipline is a willingness and commitment to do what needs to be done. Without discipline, our lives would be in disarray. Think about the things you do daily or weekly that are necessary to keep your life running smoothly. Mucking out, cleaning tack, washing rugs, grooming, checking and cleaning paddocks and maintaining your vehicle and trailer, working, bathing, paying bills, balancing the chequebook, sleeping, and more are all required activities. Without them, what would your life look like? And your horse?

If you lack self-discipline, you may find yourself procrastinating and putting your duties aside – which can create a colossal mess if you do it too frequently. Ingrained unhelpful habits and an undisciplined mind may eventually prevent you from achieving your horse riding dreams, and without some kind of inner or outer motivation, you are unlikely to develop the discipline you need.

To escape this downward spiral and develop a strong sense of self-discipline, you need to get and stay motivated! How can you do this? There are several ways, but here are few to begin with:

1. Focus on the benefits.

With every task or chore you do, spend a few moments emphasising the benefit you will receive from doing it. Why are you getting up at 5 to muck out? So that you can have time to ride this afternoon. To become and stay motivated, it is crucial to have some sort of pay-off in mind. Even if your pay-off will come at a future time, remind yourself why this task or chore is a good thing.

2. Work towards a specific, realistic goal.

Divide the goal into small steps and focus on one each day. Remind yourself that if you don't complete the steps that will create the outcome you desire, you will not meet your objective.

3. Use visualisation.

See the big picture. Remember that this task is only one part of a larger puzzle. It's hard to get inspired about cleaning tack until you envision yourself accepting the winner's trophy sitting on this very same shining, immaculate saddle. By looking at the big picture, each little task will retain a measure of importance in your mind.

4. Inspire yourself!

Put inspirational quotes and posters where you can see them often, watch inspirational films, spend time with other riders who inspire you. Read inspirational books, about horses and training and great masters...but also books written especially for equestrians who need more motivation, confidence and self-discipline. Make sure you have a trainer that inspires you...essential if you are to make any progress.

5. Set time apart every day to review your motivation and your goals. Keep a training log. Record your hopes, dreams, doubts and victories. Get yourself a life coach that works exclusively with equestrians and understands exactly how many challenges horse riders and horse owners have to face every day.

The secret of horse riding success is to invest as much time in your mental, as in your physical training.

Re-framing

Looking at your horse and your riding from a different viewpoint can be an eye opener

It is not because things are difficult that we do not dare; it is because we do not dare that they are difficult Seneca

Re-framing is a process by which a person's perception of a specific event is altered, resulting in a different emotional response. Ex.: When life deals you a lemon - make lemonade!

That's re-framing! It's the art of choosing what to give greatest significance to in any situation. Are you going to concentrate on the negative aspects and be miserable? Or are you going to find the silver lining even if it is part of a thundercloud?

In re-framing; you choose what an event will mean to you and how you are going to respond to it emotionally. You can change the emphasis from the depressing to the motivating or inspiring, and focus on that. After a dressage test, you focus intentionally on what went well, instead of what went wrong. Usually, we tend to maximise our blunders, even if they are by far in the minority. We are blind and deaf to our own successes.

Isn't this a form of denial? No, it isn't. You don't deny that something happened. You just look at it from a different angle.

So things did not go the way you had hoped.

Instead of beating yourself up about it, you choose to focus on the positive aspects, and if there aren't any, you look for something that you can learn from the experience and focus on that. No experience is ever wasted, not even a very negative one. What doesn't kill you indeed makes you stronger.

You accept that you have a choice in how you respond emotionally. You can choose to feel angry or you can choose to feel sorry for yourself. Or you can focus on what did go right or what you have learned from the situation.

We always have a choice in how we allow events to affect us. It's not the event itself that creates emotions inside us. It is our interpretation of what happened and our response to this interpretation that causes us to feel certain emotions.

Re-framing is the art actively choosing how we are going to respond. We can consciously decide not to get angry/ depressed/ resentful. We consciously decide not to judge or criticise ourselves (or our horses/ trainers/ spouses: the weather etc. etc.) and so harm our confidence.

It takes a bit of practice to master the technique and get into the habit of re-framing.

But it is worth it, you are worth it, and so is your horse! Stop feeling sorry for yourself and liberate yourself from the all-too-common tendency to consider yourself a victim of circumstances.

We all have to cope with disappointments from time to time. We all deal with disappointments in our own unique way.

Some people go into denial and then move on as if it never happened. Others withdraw, become wary or even emotionally paralysed. Yet others seem to thrive on adversity, seeing each irritation as a challenge.

Think about it for a moment... Just how do you deal with aggravation? Do you like your friends to console you? Furiously throw yourself into some activity? Or acting as if you do not care in the slightest-by shutting out any thoughts about it?

And how did you develop your way of handling emotional disturbances? Most of us have a preferred way of coping with life's little irritations – one that developed from our efforts to cope with past experiences.

My preferred technique is to "change the labels". Generally, we tend to put our memories into the broad categories of pain or pleasure.

We can diffuse a lot of our past pain by honestly looking at our categories and seeing how they can be re-labelled.

For example, let's say you are working with a computer and it crashes, destroying your day's work. How do you label the disappointment? Do you give it a destructive label like "I am no good with computers?" Or a constructive one like "In future, I will save my work more often?"

The pain you have experienced in the past can be re-labelled or re-viewed or 're-framed' as a valuable lesson or opportunity to grow. It can endow us with the qualities of caring and compassion for our fellow suffers.

In addition to the re-labelling process, there is a range of other NLP techniques that you can use to 'reprogram' (or change how you are affected by) your past. And to design a better future, since our past can determine our future unless we are careful.

Unlike many other learning systems, NLP does not provide a rigid recipe of steps that will only work under rigid conditions. Instead, it provides a box of tools that help keep you on course, positive, successful and happy.

By three methods we may learn wisdom: First, by reflection, which is noblest; second, by imitation, which is easiest; and third by experience, which is the bitterest. Confucius

Visualisation and Mental Rehearsal

The golden key to peak performance

At the end of this section, you will know how to train your imagination to help you to feel confident, serene and satisfied with your performance

What Is Visualisation/Imagery and how does it work?

Visualisation involves only one of the 5 senses: visual. It could be extended to involve all 5 your senses. Imagery is a flow of thoughts you can see, hear, feel, smell, or taste. An image is an inner representation of your experiences– a way your mind codes, stores and expresses information.

Imagery is a window on your inner world, a way of viewing your own ideas, feelings and perceptions. But it is more than a mere window– is a means of transformation that may unconsciously direct your life and shape your health.

The power of the mind to influence the body is remarkable. Your thoughts have a direct influence on the way you feel and behave. If you tend to dwell on sad or negative thoughts, you most likely are not a very happy person. Likewise, if you think that your job gives you a headache, you probably will come home with throbbing temples each day.

Imagery is the most fundamental language we use. Everything you experience is processed by the mind through one or more of the 5 senses. When we recall events from our past or childhood, it is seldom through words. It is often visual, but can also be sounds, tastes, smells or a combination of sensations. A certain smell, for example, may invoke either pleasant or unpleasant memories in you. Similarly, going to a place where you had a nasty riding accident may instantly invoke visions of the accident and initiate the flight or fight response.

Imagine holding a fresh, juicy lemon in your hand. Perhaps you can feel its texture or see the vividness of its yellow skin. As you slice it open, you see the juice squirt out of it. The lemon's tart aroma is overwhelming. Finally, you stick it in your mouth, suck on it and taste the sour flavour as the juices roll over your tongue. More than likely, your body reacted in some way to this image. You may have begun to salivate.

Imagery is the language that the mind uses to communicate with the body.

It is estimated that an average person has 10,000 thoughts or images flashing through his mind each day. At least half of those thoughts are negative, such as the anxiety before a riding competition, passing the spot where your horse always spooks, failing to master a dressage manoeuvre, etc.

Unharnessed, a steady dose of worry can alter your physiology and make you more susceptible to a variety of diseases, ranging from PMS to colds and flu, headaches to heart disease, ulcers to indigestion. However, if you can learn to direct and control the images in your head, you can change your mood. Our imagination is like a spirited, powerful horse. If it's untamed, it can be dangerous. But if you learn to use your imagination in a way that is purposeful and directed, it can be a tremendously powerful tool to get you exactly what you want.

Most proponents suggest practising for 15 to 20 minutes a day initially to ensure that you're learning to do it properly. But as you become more skilled and comfortable with the technique, you'll be able to do it for just a few minutes at a time as needed throughout the day.

Mental Rehearsal

Mental rehearsal is visualisation/imagery in action - an excellent technique to get oneself in the right state of mind to handle a challenging situation. Mental rehearsal is a simple but powerful technique that focuses and directs the imagination to facilitate improving your performance or reaching your goals.

What Mental Rehearsal Is and Why It Works

Mental rehearsal involves the mental practice of a task as opposed to actual practice. During mental rehearsal, you imagine performing a specific task without actually doing anything.

Mental rehearsal assists the skill learning process and provides the extra edge for those who have reached sufficient levels of skill development.

Why use mental rehearsal?

- It can turn a challenging situation into a "trigger" to high-quality performance.
- It reduces anxiety that interferes with your performance.
- It helps you focus and maximises confidence and creativity.
- It allows you to perfect your skills in a "no-risk" situation.

How to use mental rehearsal

1. Find a time and place where you won't be interrupted. Switch off mobile phones

2. Sit back, put your feet up or lie down, and close your eyes.

3. Relax, concentrate, and focus. Take deep breaths and exhale slowly. As you exhale, imagine that stress is leaving your body. Start at your feet ... feel all the stress leave your feet ... then your legs ... then your chest ... all the way to the top of your head ... feel all the stress leave your body. Free your mind of distractions and allow your mind to focus on the relaxation process.

Step I: Set Up

1. Once relaxed, focus on the specific performance you want to improve.

2. What are the results you are aiming for? What kind of performance would equal excellence?

Step II: Get into the appropriate mental state (mood)

1. Ask yourself, "What would be the most intense way I could possibly feel, to be at my best in this situation?"

2. Ask yourself, "What words or phrases express the ways I want to feel in this situation?"

Step III: Amplify the state

1. Start getting that ideal feeling by thinking of past experiences when you felt similarly and add words and phrases.

2. Amplify the feelings just as if you are adjusting a television/tablet/-phone: increase the brightness, volume, intensity, etc.

Step IV: The Rehearsal

Imagine the situation as if you were watching yourself in a film.

Imagine that you are performing the task and replay again and again until the film reflects an excellent performance. Concentrate on your facial expression, posture, movement, and voice.

Use all five your senses. Make it as colourful, real and intense as possible.

Imagine the perfect outcome. For example, see yourself and your horse performing at your best, then accepting the trophy. Use affirmations to strengthen the effect of the exercise. Tell yourself repeatedly that you are supremely confident and that you can perform this task successfully.

You may choose to imagine riding a dressage test or jumping a clear round. Add every possible detail: sight, sound, smells etc. Run the whole procedure through in your mind, step-by-step. Be careful to imagine yourself as an active participant, not as a passive observer. For example, to mentally rehearse show jumping, imagine that you are sitting on the horse rather than watching yourself from the gallery.

Remain relaxed and focused. Imagine going through the process and experiencing the desired, successful results. Finally, open your eyes and smile. You have practised perfectly in your mind, which is great preparation for actual performance. You will now be confident that you will perform successfully in the real situation. Remember to reward yourself for being successful. Self-re-enforcement is a great confidence booster.

This process isn't intended to build unrealistic expectations. It is designed to improve your ability to handle the real situation. You can reduce stress by visualising yourself successfully dealing with challenges. Relaxation is part of mental rehearsal exercises, and relaxation helps reduce stress.

Mental rehearsal can be used to get the very best out of yourself. It can give the confident, superior rider important practice at doing the specific actions that will be used in upcoming competitions.

When you rehearse mentally, you aren't tricking yourself into believing that you'll know what to do in competition; rather, you're giving your brain cells practise in firing some of the actual neural pathways they will follow later, in competition.

I am often asked if horse riders can benefit from self-hypnosis.

Firstly, what is Self-hypnosis?

Self-hypnosis is a process of communicating with oneself, directing one's own attention in specific ways to produce states that are commonly recognised as trance states. Neither sleep nor unconsciousness, hypnosis is a state in which a person has shut out distractions and is free to focus intently on a particular subject, emotion, or memory or goal. The hypnotic state is an optimum state for making changes in your attitude and approach to horse riding.

Why would a horse rider want to change their attitude or approach?

Because her competition nerves are hindering her performance during contests

Because she wants to get rid of the debilitating residual fear after a horse riding accident

Because she wants to get rid of ingrained riding habits that limit her progress

Because she wants to master new riding skills faster

Because she wants to stay motivated to reach her riding goals

Self-hypnosis can be a very powerful tool in the mental skills toolbox of the rider.

However, if you think hypnosis is no more than a stage trick or is performed only by charlatans, your doubts will impede any positive results that you may get from a hypnotic session. Therefore, you must be open-minded to some degree to the possibility that you can improve your riding ability through the power of auto-suggestion.

In reality, trance states are nothing special; we go in and out of these states several times during the day. Daydreaming, a well-known trance state, is a form of self-hypnosis. You have hypnotised yourself when you drive to work on auto-pilot. Afterwards, you remember little of the journey, but if you suddenly had to react fast to avoid an accident, you would have. You are not asleep during hypnosis. You are aware of everything that is being said. You can remember everything afterwards.

True, effective self-hypnosis should be designed and created by the very person who will ultimately use and benefit from it, incorporating the precise words and phrases that mean the most to that particular person. If someone is willing to take the time and mental discipline necessary to improve their riding ability and awareness of themselves and their horses, with self-hypnosis, the results will be extraordinary, positive and lasting.

Hypnosis is simply a state of mind, in much the same way that happiness is a state of mind.

Contrary to what most people believe, the mind under hypnosis is still alert and very much in control. If you cannot hear anything, then you cannot benefit from self-hypnosis. Hypnosis is a state of heightened awareness. You remain fully alert.

Anyone can be hypnotised. It is often a learned trait. You can teach your body and mind to go into a trance and get better and better at it as you practise self-hypnosis. We are constantly hypnotising ourselves. Sometimes we are our own worst enemy, when we call ourselves names, or put ourselves down and reinforce fears and limitations. It can become a habit and, if you do it long enough, you will develop a belief that will get the results you fear. Ex:

* Boy, my jumping is getting bad
* I am so bad at setting the horse up for a jump

* I will never jump higher than 90 cm, never
* My riding is really going downhill

These are auto-suggestions or negative affirmations. More appropriate auto-suggestions to give yourself under self-hypnosis would be:

* My jumping is getting better and better every day
* I am very good at show-jumping, it is easy for me to set up my horse for a jump
* I will easily jump higher than 90cm

....and because the trance state gives you direct access to your unconscious mind, you will embrace these suggestions without reserve and accept them as the pure, unadulterated truth.

Imagine what might happen if you changed the suggestions that you give yourself daily? If you used the hypnotic trance state to give yourself empowering suggestions to improve your riding, reduce your anxiety about and exponentially increase your self-esteem?

Do you tend to let your circumstances and the people around you set the tone for every day? Do you allow people and events to trigger feelings of anger, frustration and impatience or happiness, joy and contentment?

When you first wake up in the morning, spend 10 minutes thinking about the events and situations you would like to experience that day. How would you like your day to go? What kind of people would you like to meet? Would you like to receive some great opportunities to advance your career? How would you like to feel for the majority of the day? Calm, excited, appreciated, optimistic?

Spend a few minutes vividly imagining each desired scenario in your mind, exactly as you would like it to happen. Athletes do this – mental rehearsal – to prepare them to excel. Use all 5 your senses and add emotion to the exercise. And always add at the end "This or something even better!"

Most importantly, see, hear, feel, taste and smell the events as if it is actually happening now. Immerse yourself in feelings of excitement, joy, happiness and gratitude as you enjoy one great experience after another.

By the time you're finished, you will be feeling fantastic; buzzing with good spirits and high expectations!

During the day, continue with your normal routine. Do not consciously wait for things to happen as you imagined them. Simply open the door when opportunity knocks. Keep affirming that great things are going to happen to you that day and that you feel great and grateful for all of the blessings and abundance in your life already.

Eradicate feelings of worry, anxiety, frustration, and anger throughout the day because these useless feelings will interfere with the positive energy you are radiating.

Using this process on a daily basis, you'll eventually start to notice that rather amazing things happen regularly to you, as if purely by coincidence. You will often find yourself in the "right place at the right time" and be surprised by your sudden, lasting good fortune. The surprising truth is that you can decide to be happy NOW – even if not everything in your life is perfect.

Gratitude Attitude

Start by feeling grateful.

Gratitude is one of the most powerful states of mind that you can possibly adopt. Not only does it make you feel good, it shifts your focus from what you don't have to what you DO have, and keeps it there! And stop running around like a headless chicken. If you spend most of your days feeling rushed and scatter-brained, feeling happy, and content is going to be a hard act to follow.

To be truly happy, you need to make time for yourself to relax, to dream, and to re-charge your batteries. If you believe that once you "get there" everything will be perfect and you'll finally be happy, you are deluding yourself. Celebrate every single moment that you are alive, starting now. Make the journey worthwhile and you'll savour the result so much more!

The most important thing to understand about happiness is that it is largely a CHOICE you make from moment to moment. Embrace happiness, and allow it will grow to gigantic proportions in your life!

Time Management

Finally...

We rush through one thing so we can get to the next. We can't wait for Christmas to be over so we can start getting ready for Valentine's Day. There might be snow outside, but we're already thinking about the beach in the summer. In our society, we experience a certain pressure to finish as much as possible in the shortest amount of time - all in the name of efficiency. But what happens when you're so wrapped up in the big finish that you don't pay attention during the race itself? You miss the experience and learning of the journey.

Effective time management is a challenge in itself. I have found a few strategies that work for me and share them with you below:

1 Prioritise.

Keep a diary to plan your daily activities. Organise and Prioritise. Trying to do everything at once is impossible. You will feel overwhelmed, and, as a result, you may not accomplish anything. Do the worst and hardest tasks first. Keep your to-do list and calendar with you at all times. If you fail to plan, you plan to fail. Allocate a specific amount of time for a particular task and keep to that.

Prioritising your responsibilities and engagements is crucial. If you do not prioritise, you will become known as a procrastinator. A 1, 2, 3 - to do list places items in order of importance. This type of list is divided into three sections: 1, 2, or 3. The items placed in the 1 section are those needed to be done that day. The items placed in the 2 section need completion within the week. The 3 section items are those things that need to be done within the month. As the 2 and 3 items become more pertinent, they are bumped up to the 1 or 2 list.

There is always enough time for the most important things. If it is important, you should be able to make time for it. Ask yourself WHY are you doing something? Define your needs, goals, hopes, and dreams. What is your motivation? The more you understand why you are doing what you are, the less stress and the more time you will have. If you cannot come up with a good reason, then stop wasting your time.

2. Learn to say no.

Politely saying no should be an ingrained habit. Saying no frees up time for the things that are more important. Just say no. Focus on your own goals, not your spouse's or children's or parents' or employer's. Know yourself, your dreams, your passions, and your life's purpose. Saying no is one of the hardest things in life, but will help make you a success of everything you set out to achieve.

3. Don't be a perfectionist.

Nobody is perfect. You should set achievable goals, but they should also be challenging. If you are struggling to carry out all the tasks you feel you are supposed to do, then talk to someone who might be able to advise you. Explain the difficulties and ask for their suggestions or help.

4. Make time to relax.

Do not overwork yourself. Life's too short. Resist the temptation to schedule things back-to-back. All too often, we underestimate how long things will take. Schedule time for both work and play. Working too much or for too long, uninterrupted hours is inefficient and can lead to burnout. Too often we tell ourselves we don't "have time" or can't "make time" to relax and have fun.

While we can't "make" a day last longer than 24 hours, each of us starts the day with exactly the same number of hours. Take a part of your time to acknowledge the good things in your life. Practise the Gratitude Attitude. Work hard but know when to take time off to be with the family, go for a hack, or read a book. This dissipates stress and slows down your heart rate, allows you to digest food normally, and empowers your immune system.

5. Delegate

Knowing yourself and your limits may be one of the most important ways to manage time effectively. When you need help, get help. A major source of inefficient time management is trying to control events or people over whom you have little or no power.

When confronted with a stressful situation, when you have little time to deal with it, ask yourself: is this really my problem? If it isn't, leave it alone. If it is, can you resolve it now?

Once the problem is settled, move on. Don't agonise over the decision. Try to accept situations you cannot change. There are many circumstances in life beyond your control. Know your limits. If a problem is beyond your control and cannot be changed at the moment, don't fight the situation. And ask for help when you need it. Getting the help you need is in itself a major time management tip! Master the art of appropriate DELEGATION.

6. Take time to breathe properly.

Running out of time often causes us to breathe shallowly, and this almost always causes more stress. Shallow breathing results in less oxygen in the bloodstream, less oxygen to the brain, reducing the ability to think clearly and increasing muscle tension. You may experience headaches; you may feel more anxious and uptight.

Take a deep breath and count to ten (or more if the situation warrants it!) Breathe in through your nose and out through your mouth. Try to inhale deep enough so that your lower abdomen rises and falls. Exhale - slowly! Stand up and stretch. Remember that relaxation is the opposite of stress. Smile. It will make you feel better! Take a short walk. If you're at work, go to the loo or get a glass of water. Do something different. When you return to the problem, chances are it won't seem nearly as insurmountable.

7. Don't self-medicate

Be wary of self-medicating with caffeine - even though it is a stimulant drug that keeps you awake when you "run out of time" - it can also alter your mood and make you feel stressed and anxious. And don't be tempted to self-medicate by drinking alcohol to relieve stress or anxiety either- alcohol is a depressant drug that can make you feel low, despite its apparent initial relaxing effects.

Alcohol and other drugs do not provide you with extra time nor remove the conditions that cause stress. Although they may seem to offer temporary relief, these substances only mask or disguise problems. Prescription medications should be taken only on the advice of your doctor.

Have a cup of herbal tea instead. Most of us know about the calming properties of chamomile tea. But a steaming cup of red bush, catnip, passionflower, skullcap or kava kava also work very well. Use tea bags or loose tea (one teaspoon of tea per cup of boiling water). Allow the flavour to develop for about 10 minutes to get the full benefits of the herbs.

Keep a training log – this is how you measure and monitor your horse riding confidence level

Supremely confident riders keep training logs to monitor their progress and build their self-esteem by reviewing past successes.

I do realise that most of you are convinced that you have neither the time nor the aptitude to indulge in something as frivolous as keeping a diary. Serious riders do not waste precious riding time on writing sweet nothings in pink, lockable diaries, right?

Wrong. Serious riders keep training logs.

Your aim is to be supremely confident. The single, most empowering action you can take right now is to start a Training Log. Not just to trace your training progress but also to record your feelings, triumphs, disappointments and insights. As well as helping you to realise your riding goals and ambitions, a personal training log has been proven to be an effective self-help tool which can also improve your emotional and physical health.

In earlier generations, it was common practice to keep a diary or personal journal. Today very few people still do it, no one has the time. This is a great pity. If you can read and write, you have access to one of the most amazing sources of personal power! Try it for 30 days, and it will transform your life! Clients periodically tell me they couldn't possibly find the time. Just try it for 30 days. You'll soon find that you couldn't possibly live without the power of your journals.

The benefits of a training log for self-doubting riders

It helps you set and track your goals, sort- and long-term. It helps you to remain focused and motivated - Writing in your log creates more personal awareness, and therefore helps you to concentrate on the issues that are important to you. A journal will clarify your goals. As you write a few thoughts each day, your ideas about what is important, what is worthy of your life and your time will become much clearer. You'll automatically discover what you really want in life.

It helps you get organised! - Logging your goals and what you want to accomplish for the day, the month, the year, or a lifetime is an excellent tool to help you get those things done.

The distance is nothing; it is only the first step that is difficult. ~Marie de Vichy-Chamrond, Marquise du Deffand, letter to Jean Le Rond d'Alembert, 7 July 1763

It reduces stress so that you are more likely to be successful, and so increase your self-confidence. You can make short notes about your horse, your trainer, your fear, your frustration; your loss of confidence- anything that caused a strong emotional reaction. Our emotions affect us (mind, body, and soul) - either in a positive or negative way. The simple act of writing this down will allow you to gain perspective on emotional reactions.

A journal will simplify your life. Spending as little as 10 minutes with pen and paper describing your values, noting your achievements and giving thanks for the joys of life, will make you less tolerant of life's distractions.

A journal will empower you. Thinking with pen and paper forces you to eliminate fuzzy or confusing images and "laser" in on precisely the right word, the most powerful image to express yourself.

It helps you sleep better! Writing down the things that are "on your mind", gives your brain permission to let go, and induces more restful sleep. Making a list of the things you were grateful for that day, however small and simple, will soothe and re-assure you.

It is the record of your riding life. When keeping a log, you record your riding experiences, dreams, ideas, desires, thoughts and more, for reflecting on now, and in the future.

It helps you to understand and accept yourself, your horse and others. Awareness of the past can teach and support you in the future. You are creating a record that will make it easier to see patterns, changes, and shifts. It will become a precious keepsake, an eternal legacy.

Acknowledge Your Achievements!

Chances are, you've achieved several goals during the past 6 months. Did you stop, feel the sense of accomplishment, and take time to celebrate? Or did you immediately move on to the next big project? It's never too late for a celebration. Reward yourself, like you would your horse, and remind yourself of what you have achieved. No, you are not overindulgent - you are practising the art of gratitude and attracting even more success into your life by acknowledging that good things do happen to everyone.

Conclusion

Congratulations! You have reached the end of your HORSE RIDING CONFIDENCE SECRETS book.

You have discovered how to acknowledge and accept your fear, set smart goals, why it is important to keep a diary, how to get rid of your limiting beliefs, use affirmations, anchors and mental rehearsal to increase your riding confidence and learn more effectively.

Ending with Equestrian Humour

Horse people need a healthy sense of humour. Our five senses are not enough to cope with the demands of owning and caring for our horses. We need an extra one: a well-developed sense of humour. Nurturing our sense of humour will help us cope with every challenging situation we are confronted with, even the very worst.

We have to keep our sense of humour fit and healthy, we have to exercise it with enthusiasm several times a day. Find something that makes you laugh. Anything. A film, a book, a stand-up comedian, a poster, a horse... Not only do horse people desperately need a sense of humour, but their families are doomed without it. Below an exercise program to get your sense of humour fit in 15 'easy' steps:

Start by smiling a bit more often. Smile at yourself in the mirror, smile at your horse in his stable, smile at the sight of foals frolicking in the field.

Rent some DVD's and have a laughter-orgy/ Monty Python, the Full Monty, Fools and Horses, Blazing Saddles, Men in Tights etc. etc.

Learn how to laugh at yourself, alone and in the presence of other people. Instead of cringing, try to see the humorous side. Especially at the very moment- laugh while you are still covered in mud from top to toe.

Laugh at life's little annoyances. One way to do that: Think about it as if it happened to someone else, someone you like – or maybe someone you don't. Laugh at him, then laugh at yourself!

Try not to take every slight personally. Diffuse a difficult situation with humour. Do not take offence too easily, everyone has bad days, you too.

Make a point of noticing something funny every day. What happened today that brought a smile to your face or made you laugh?

Do something silly, something completely out of character. Learn a few good, clean jokes, and tell them with jest. Making other people laugh is nearly as good as laughing yourself. Laughing is infectious, impossible to keep a straight face.

Connect with Horses Workshops

PS. Shameless Self-Promotion
(with apologies from the author)

Should you feel like combining personal development with a holiday in one of the most beautiful parts of France, you can always join us for a personal empowerment workshop here on the farm.

The Connect with Horses Mindfulness Workshops

My Twitter profile says I am a "recycled MD, a writer and mindfulness and meditation workshop presenter." In a nutshell, that is about right. You already know that I am a writer. In addition to this book, you may also have read French Women's Confidence Secrets, the first book in the Fabriqué en France series. If not, you can read the second chapter at the end of this book. I also present Connect with Horses one, five and seven-day workshops.

You may have noticed a couple of not-so-subtle references to my workshops in this book. You may have wondered what it is all about, especially Equine-assisted Experiential Learning (EEL) and equine-assisted personal empowerment. Did I mention EEL? I am sure I did. I must have — several times. You may even, in desperation, have clicked on an EEL link and you may already now know what EEL is.

The reason I mention the workshops so often is that one of the best ways to find out more about equine guided mindfulness meditation and equine-assisted personal empowerment is to try it out in person, in the presence of horses. (For those of you who love horses and who would love to spend some time with them but cannot do so in person, for whatever reason, at this moment in time, I have written the book Mindfulness and Meditation Options. You can access it at my author website MargarethaMontagu.com)

Each of the chapters in this book starts with an e-mail, a text or a telephone call that I received from a potential workshop participant. I couldn't very well NOT mention the workshops. If these rather too frequently-occurring references are starting to get on your nerves, I apologise. I will stop doing it immediately. At the end of this chapter, you will know everything you ever wanted to know about my Connect with Horses workshops.

I initially created these workshops because I am obsessed with helping people manage stress more effectively. Mindfulness and meditation can help you deal better with stress. It can help you avoid the physical and mental damage that stress can cause. That is why I set out to write this book, to help people manage stress with mindfulness and meditation. It was just going to be a standard "Find the right meditation method for you" book. As you may have gathered, my horses had other ideas.

Why would you want to attend a Connect with Horses Personal Development workshop?

Right, this chapter is supposed to be about my workshops. So, the idea of the workshops is to offer participants the chance to get away from the challenges and demands of everyday life. When you attend one of my workshops here in the south of France, you will have time to rest, to reflect and to recharge your batteries. You will be able to leave the complexity of your daily life behind, with all its demands, deadlines, doubts and disagreements. You will be encouraged to:

- put yourself first without feeling guilty,
- discover or re-discover your life's purpose,
- uncover your full potential,
- spend time "being" rather than "doing,"
- de-stress and learn how to manage stress more effectively,
- re-connect with your authentic self,
- look at your life from a distance and a different perspective,
- eradicate limiting beliefs that hold you back,
- get rid of unhealthy habits,
- make new, like-minded friends,
- exchange your inner critic for an inner cheerleader,
- spend time enjoying the beauty of nature,
- boost your creativity,
- find inspiration and motivation to make permanent changes,
- investigate mindfulness and meditation as effective stress management strategies,
- choose the meditation technique that works best for you
- focus on what is important to you,
- forget about the shopping you need to do, the food you need to cook, the dishes you need to wash,
- experiment with leaving your comfort zone,
- say what you want to say without having to worry about the consequences,
- rebuild your shattered self-image,
- process past experiences,
- count your blessings,
- sleep peacefully and undisturbed for as long as you need to,
- stop making excuses
- and just be YOU.

"Thanks again for sharing your life with us! I had such a wonderful time at your place and in your company. I feel revitalised, relaxed and blessed. All

the best and big hugs for the two of you and all the cats, horses and dog." E.G. Meijling

"A powerful and wonderful life experience, with caring guidance. One can truly experience a mindful meditation with the horses who are definitely spiritual. Also, your senses become reinvigorated with the beautiful food and wine, while sitting and listening to the unique sound of nature's calmness." S. Murphy

Thank you so much for the beautiful day on Saturday. It was a truly special and treasurable experience that I feel very lucky to have had. Your horses are such lovely characters, and it was fun getting to know them a little. They have stayed in my mind. I would love to come back again sometime. B. Garcias. (Touched by a Horse one-day-workshop)

A substantial number of you will read this book, start a gratitude and generosity journal and cope with change more effectively. A small number of you will find the idea of establishing a gratitude and generosity habit while staying in one of the most beautiful parts of France irresistible. Eh bien, you are soooooo very welcome here if you feel the need to get away from all the hustle-and-bustle, not only to rest but also to be able to concentrate fully on what you want to achieve. These workshops offer you the opportunity to deepen your awareness of yourself, of other people, of horses and the world around you. These workshops are personal transformational workshops that can be life-changing experiences.

This is where Equine-assisted Experiential Learning, the foundation of Equine-assisted Personal Empowerment, comes in.

My workshops aim to enable women (and a few men too along the way) to put the principles described in this book into practice with the help of our horses. These personal empowerment workshops are unique because they offer participants the opportunity to discover equine-assisted experiential learning (EEL) and equine-guided mindfulness meditation.

EEL will help you:

- free yourself from immobilising fear and so dramatically increase your self-confidence,
- discover simple techniques to deal with stressful situations effectively
- communicate more efficiently and with more assertiveness,
- find out how to accept and appreciate yourself,
- strengthen and deepen relationships at work and home,
- eradicate limiting beliefs and replace them with empowering beliefs,
- develop more successful problem-solving skills,
- thrive on change and challenges and
- gain a solid understanding of who you are now.

Having thus substantially increased your self-confidence, you could

- leave your dead-end job and find a much better one,
- ask for that raise you know you deserve,
- start the business you have always dreamed of owning,
- go back to school and get the qualifications you want,
- build stable relationships with your significant other, your parents, your children, your friends and family...

Do you feel over-burdened by the trials and tribulations of life? Do you feel physically exhausted and mentally strangled and desperately long to escape? Would you like to develop more successful problem-solving skills, communicate more effectively, build healthier relationships and significantly increase your self-confidence? If you do, then a **Connect with Horses** workshop in the sun-drenched south of France may be what you need to help you put the principles discussed in this book into practice.

The Connect with Horses workshops offer you:

-an affordable escape from the always escalating demands of everyday life,

-easy access via 5 international airports, served by low-cost airlines, less than 2 hours' drive from the retreat

-a safe haven in one of the most beautiful parts of France, secluded but not isolated, a place where you can rest and sleep undisturbed for as long as you need to

-fresh air, clean water and scrumptious home-cooked and mostly home-grown food to nourish both your body and your mind

Participants leave our farm here in the south of France with a profound sense of contentment and satisfaction, full of energy and feeling fit, healthy and supremely confident. And where better can one discover and test-drive your new skills than amongst our sun-drenched vineyards in a private, secure and beautiful setting?

This unique and unforgettable workshop in the sun-baked south of France was created exclusively for discerning horse riders who want more from a holiday: a life-changing equine-assisted adventure!

If you are looking for a purely relaxing spa retreat, spending your days detoxing and being pampered, then a Connect with Horses personal empowerment workshop is not for you. If you want to relax and get away from it all, but you also want to take a good look at who you are now and where you want to go from here, then one of my workshops would be a good investment in your well being. Participants attend 1/3/5/7-day workshops. To find out more, visit EquineGuidedGrowth.com or e-mail me on at welcome2gascony@gmail.com.

Free Preview

Self-Confidence Made Simple
16 Frenchwomen share their Self-esteem Secrets
Available at MargarethaMontagu.com
ISBN: 9782956732402
Publisher: SemperEquuS

To give my readers a sneak preview of one of my other books, the first book in the Fabriqué en France series, Self-Confidence Made Simple – 16 Frenchwomen share their Self-esteem Secrets.

French women are famous for their effortless elegance, their enchanting independence, their irresistible charm and their unshakable self-confidence.

In my book, Self-Confidence Made Simple: 16 Frenchwomen share their Self-esteem Secrets, a handful of my closest French friends share their confidence secrets with you. I have lived in France for part of my childhood and most of my adult life. I have spent nearly twenty-five years, first as a medical doctor and more recently as a workshop leader, empowering women to live long, happy, healthy and fulfilling lives, full of purpose and meaning. It's my life's mission.

As you share these women's joys and sorrows, you will discover how they remain unconditionally self-confident, serenely sophisticated and perfectly poised no matter how challenging the situations are that they find themselves in. To each story and every secret, I have added my (by now) extensive knowledge and experience, with practical suggestions to help you incorporate each of these potentially life-changing strategies into your own life.

Self-Confidence Made Simple is a guide to becoming a woman who knows exactly who she is, who takes excellent care of herself, who leads a balanced, purposeful and fulfilling life, who has a reliable support network, who can laugh at herself, who knows she has a lot to be grateful for, who knows how to forgive, who competently handles stress, who knows how to say NO without apologising and who knows that being ageless is all about attitude.

If you too want to master the skills you need to develop rock-solid self-confidence, this book is for you. Below you will find an extract from the book, to give you an idea of how it can help you dramatically increase your self-confidence.

Content

French women are confident:

- Because they know how to look after themselves - Chapter 1 Sumptuous Self-Care
- Because they know who they are - Chapter 2 Choosing and Changing Your Identity
- Because they know how to keep their lives in balance - Chapter 3 Balancing Act
- Because they have extensive support systems - Chapter 4 Rock-solid Support Systems
- Because they never forget how much they have to be grateful for - Chapter 5 Gratitude and Generosity
- Because they know how to deal with stress and make it work for them - Chapter 6 Taming and Harnessing Stress

• Because they do not allow resentment to erode their confidence - Chapter 7 Forgiveness

• Because they know age is just a number - Chapter 8 Confronting Age

Implementing the French Approach - Chapter 9

Links to: Self-care Quiz, Self-Confidence Quiz, Self-Criticism Quiz, Stress Quiz, Vision Board Guide, Creative Visualisation Guide

About the book and what it can do for you

With the help of my five horses, I host personal empowerment workshops at our house here in the south of France. More than one of our guests has commented on the unflappable confidence of the local women. They also seem to be under the impression that French women are more confident than women from other nationalities. I am not convinced that this is true. I decided to look into the way French women approach life to see if their approach is different and to see whether this different approach results in them being exceptionally confident. My main aim with this book is to entertain my readers and if a few pearls of wisdom slip into the text, so much the better. The last chapter does give clear guidelines about how to go about adopting the French approach, but it is the only part of the book that is directive. The rest of the book is full of suggestions, but this is not a step-by-step guide of what to do if you want to boost your self-confidence. I believe in "showing," rather than "telling." I think today's women are perfectly aware that there is no one-size-fits-all solution to confidence building. They know that a technique that works for one person may fail miserably for another. This book puts several possible options before you, enabling you to decide for yourself what will work for you and what not.

Each chapter looks at one possible reason why French women may be markedly more confident. I was not born in France, but I have spent part of my childhood here and most of my adulthood. I have a fair amount of experience of the French savoir-faire. In each chapter, I discuss the subject with one of my French friends. I also share some of my own experiences in each chapter. There may also be a few suggestions of how you can incorporate these strategies into your own life, should you choose to do so.

I have created a Playlist on YouTube that you can listen to while you read. It is a collection of French chansons, sung by French chanteuses. Some are older, like Edith Piaf's "Non, je ne regrette rien" and some are more recent like Jennifer's "Tourner ma page." Some are controversial, like Mylene Farmer's "Je te dis tout," some are full of nostalgia like Barbara Patin's "L'Aigle Noir," and some are just about politically correct like Carla Bruni's "Quelqu'un m'a dit."

Choosing and Changing your Identity

My understanding of self-confidence is simple. You are a confident person when you know you can handle any challenge that comes your way. You know that you are wise enough, competent enough, experienced enough and intelligent enough to cope with most situations. Knowing this would imply that you know yourself well. You are intimately acquainted with your strengths as well as your weaknesses. Not all of us are.

Many French women seem to have an unfair advantage in this regard. Many of the confident French women I am privileged to call my friends have a clear understanding of who they are. Ask any of them. You will immediately, in no uncertain terms, without any hesitation, and with complete confidence be told that they are, first and foremost, 100% French. They are Gascons (from the Gascony region of France). They are from such and such a village where their family has lived for the last five centuries, at least. Go ahead and ask them how they would describe themselves. They will tell you that as French women, they are independent, courageous and highly intelligent. As Gascon women, they are loyal, spontaneous, generous and full of joie de vivre. As a Garreau, Maillard or Ducasse women, they are intelligent, determined and sympathetic. Knowing who you are and what you are capable of can be a great advantage in a stressful situation.

I asked my friend Anaïs, who is serenely confident in all situations, how she manages to be so sure of herself at all times. She explained:

"If I am confident, it is because I know who I am. I grew up in a small village in the Gers. I was brought up by both my parents. Mostly by my mother, as Papa was always busy with the farm. I did not see that much of him. I grew up surrounded by both sets of grandparents, my mother's sister and of her children and my father's brothers and their children. In the same small village, my grandfather's family lived. He had two sisters. Their children and grandchildren lived in our village too.

I had no problem when I was a teenager to figure out who I am. I am Anaïs K, daughter of Jacques and Edith K, granddaughter of Babette and Jean K, sister of Lucas K and cousin of Thierry, Amelie, Marie-Claire and Genevieve.

Our family has lived in the village for many generations, so I was also Anaïs K. from Fenton, a village in the Gers. A Gersois, born and bred and proud of the fact. Gersois people are often convivial, hospitable, passionate, intense and sometimes short-tempered. Knowing this, I also had a good idea of what sort of person I am.

The men and women of my family took part in all the wars that ravaged in this region. We fought in the war against the Black Prince in the 13th century and in all the wars since then, including the Great War. Several members of my family died during the Second World War – both in the front lines and in the service of the Resistance. We are known and respected in the region because of the sacrifices we made. I know I come from courageous, tenacious and strong-willed stock. This helps me when I find myself in challenging situations.

My family has farmed this land for centuries. They were, and are, careful and conscientious farmers. They took good care of the land so that their sons and grandsons would benefit from their investment. We are a family of winemakers. I grew up close to the land. I knew from an early age that there would be a place for me on the farm for the rest of my life.

I am a vigneron's daughter. I learnt the art from my father, my grandfather and my uncles. I also learnt from my mother and my aunts, who looked after the finances and marketing of our wine business. I always loved this way of life, the countryside, the Gers and the people who live here. As you know, my brother is today a lecturer at Pau University, so I took over my father's vineyard. The part of the farm that my father inherited from my grandfather was small. My father managed to buy more land and planted more vines. This means I make a comfortable living doing something I adore and have loved since I was a child. Since most of my family still live in the village, I never have to go far if I need advice about anything! Sometimes we disagree because I want to use newer methods of wine producing. If they give me too much hassle, I remind them that they used to be called rebel-vignerons in their youth!

Living in a village surrounded by my own family meant that I always had friends close by. Several of my cousins were the same age as I was or a couple of years older or younger. I have heard it said that one's cousins are often the first friends one has in life. That was the case in my life. We were all blessed with the same genes. We had many physical and mental characteristics in common. Many mannerisms too. It not only gave me a sense of who I am but also a sense of belonging. As some of my cousins were older than I was, I always had a choice of role models. Most of my childhood friends also had a clear understanding of who they were and what they were good at. We took this knowledge for granted.

My mother saw early on which way the wind was blowing. She realised that my brother was not interested in taking over the farm. He wanted to study and become an academic. She realised that I was the one who wanted to become a winemaker, so she prepared the way for me. I cannot say that there wasn't any opposition when my father and uncles realised a woman was going to take over my father's estate. I did have a few things going for me: I am a vigneron's daughter. Wine making is in my blood. I have learnt everything there is to know about wine making from my father and my uncles. I learnt about the finances and marketing of wine from my mother and aunts. I had the enthusiasm my brother lacked. Eventually, I won the battle. My generation's women have to prove that women can make wine as well as any man. The next generation's women will be accepted as equals, if not better winemakers than men.

You see, the fact that I know who I am makes me confident in my abilities. This knowledge has served me well, making my way in life and getting to do what I love to do.

I do not know if this type of confidence, based on a clear understanding of one's own identity, is exclusive to Frenchwomen. What I do know is that it has helped several women of my generation convince our own families, and the public at large, that we are as good at making and selling wine as our fathers and forefathers were."

What can you do if you did not grow up with this in-bred knowledge of who you are and where you come from? There is a way you can develop this sort of confidence. You can create your own identity.

It has been said that life is less about finding yourself and more about creating or recreating yourself. This makes sense to me. I think that having a strong sense of your own unique identity affects how confident you are.

Defining Your Identity

The rest of this chapter shows you, step-by-step, how to define (or re-define) precisely who you want to be. Having a clear-cut understanding of who you are, provides you with a solid foundation to build on. If you lack confidence in yourself, you can start rebuilding your confidence by laying a strong foundation - an unambiguous understanding of who you are.

End of Preview

This book will empower you to

- make quick decisions in stressful situations based on what is important to you
- accept yourself and appreciate your unique talents and abilities
- believe in yourself so that you can make the changes you want to make in your life
- deal with stress before it damages your physical or mental health
- care for yourself physically, mentally and spiritually
- build strong, long-lasting relationships
- create a stable and reliable support network so that you can
- ask for help before you feel overwhelmed
- set firm boundaries and say NO without feeling guilty or needing to explain
- focus on what you can learn from an experience
- realise that whatever age you are at is the best age for you to be

- stop criticising yourself and
- celebrate your success without needing to apologise for being brilliant

And much, much more...

Buy your own copy directly from my website MargarethaMontagu.com or from Amazon or Barnes and Noble, Kobo, Nook and iApple

www.ingramcontent.com/pod-product-compliance
Ingram Content Group UK Ltd.
Pitfield, Milton Keynes, MK11 3LW, UK
UKHW041851190726
13854UKWH00002B/839